Project Omaha Beach

Project Omaha Beach

The Life and Military Service of a Penobscot Indian Elder

Charles Norman Shay *4 Oct, 2019*

Dedicated to Bill and Rikki,
From, Charles Norman Shay
Former member: 1ST. U.S. Infantry Division
16th Infantry Regiment
medic with "F" Company, 2nd Battalion
landed on "Omaha Beach" at 06:30 AM
06·06·1944

Polar Bear & Company
Solon, Maine

Charles Norman Shay's website: www.charlesnormanshay.com
First hardcover edition 2013
First paperback edition 2012

 Polar Bear & Company™ is an imprint of
the Solon Center for Research and Publishing
PO Box 311, Solon, Maine 04979 U.S.A.
207.643.2795, www.polarbearandco.org

Library of Congress Control Number: 2011941298
ISBN 978-1-882190-08-9

Cover Design by Ramona du Houx and Carole Duval
Map page 206 from *Above the Gravel Bar: The Native Canoe Routes of Maine*, courtesy of the author, David S. Cook. Penobscot turtle emblem and illustrations by James Eric Francis Sr. Photo credits: Cover photo of Normandy beach, Ian Patrick, ianpatrickimages.com; Cantigny and European portion of the first visit, Harald Prins and Bunny McBride; page 136 Jean Jaques Sentucq; page 137 Jean-Daniel Chopin; page 192 Bangor Daily News; pages 162, 196-7, 204 Paul Cornell du Houx; page 207 Ramona du Houx; all other photos courtesy of Jean Renault and photographers from the Association Béarn-Acadie-Nouvelle France, and the author.

Manufactured on acid-free paper in more than one country.

Contents

Foreword

CHARLES SHAY, HARALD PRINS, AND BUNNY MCBRIDE

On a visit to the Penobscot Indian Reservation in the summer of 2004, we stopped, as usual, to pay our respects to tribal elder Charles Shay, who had just marked his 80th birthday. Even before crossing the bridge to Indian Island, one can easily spot his red-roofed white house and towering wooden teepee among the trees lining the shore. Charles greeted us at the door, impeccably dressed—looking every inch the cosmopolitan gentleman he has become in the course of an adventurous life, much of it spent far away from home.

Charles's house on the reservation once belonged to his aunt Lucy Nicolar, better known to the public as Princess Watahwaso. She lived here with her Kiowa Indian husband, Bruce Poolaw, from 1930 until her death in 1969. For decades, this couple made headlines across the country as famous performers of Indian songs, dances and stories. During Charles's growing-up years, he was often in their home. And, like numerous other children on the reservation, he frequently participated in their public performances. The two-story wooden teepee was constructed several years after Charles was drafted into the U.S. Army in 1943. Lucy and Bruce had it built to house their Indian basketry and novelty store, which quickly became a landmark.

In the 1980s, following Lucy's death and Bruce's eventual return to his native Oklahoma, their property fell to Charles. At the time, Charles lived in Vienna, Austria, where he had met and married the love of his life, Lilli, a few years after World War II. So, over the next two decades he and his Austrian wife returned to Indian Island each summer and devoted themselves to renovating the house and teepee. In 2003, they settled in to stay, making Indian Island their year-round residence, as it had been for Charles in his childhood. By this time, Charles had turned the old teepee into a small family museum, open seasonally.

Sadly, upon their return, Lilli fell seriously ill. On our visit that year, we could not help but admire the loving skills with which Charles took care of his dying wife. During our 2004 visit the following summer, Charles proudly showed us the lovely final resting place he had created for her in a peaceful corner of his garden by the river. Understandably, he was in a particularly reflective mood that year and touched on aspects of his life that we had not talked about before. He told us how disappointed he was to have missed out on the 60th anniversary commemoration of D-Day in Normandy. Knowing nothing about his role in the war, we asked, "Were you there on D-Day?"

"Yes," he said, quietly.

"At Omaha Beach?"

Again, the same answer. Those few words—"D-Day" at "Omaha"—spoke volumes about a subject Charles had kept locked up for six decades. Feeling sorry that he had missed the opportunity to return to the landing beaches in French Normandy in the supportive company of other surviving veterans of the 1st Infantry Division (the Big Red One), we spontaneously told him we would take him there on one of our next trips to Europe, as we regularly cross the Atlantic to see relatives and friends or for professional reasons.

Over the next three years, Charles relayed, by bits and pieces, stories of his military experiences in World War II, the Korean War, and the Cold War. Like our Dutch relatives and millions of other Europeans, we gratefully remember how American, British, and Canadian allies liberated not only France and Belgium from brutal German occupation, but also our own repressed people in the Netherlands. In this struggle, they were joined by brave fighters in regional resistance movements, including Harald's father.

Hundreds of thousands of North American soldiers, including thousands of young Native tribesmen like Charles, were asked to pay the ultimate price, and many did.

Today, tens of thousands who lost their lives abroad are buried in enormous war cemeteries on the seacoast of Normandy, in the rough wilderness of the Ardennes, in the hills above the Rhine near Arnhem, and near other epic battlefields in Europe.

By spring 2007, we began to realize that it was time to make good on our offer, for Charles was nearly eighty-three years old and life is not eternal. Preparing for the journey, our communication with Charles intensified, as did background research, which focused especially on the roles American Indians played in the war. It became increasingly evident to all three of us that the planned journey was about more than one old man's personal trip into the past; it was a journey emblematic of the undocumented experiences of all Native war veterans of the Penobscot and other Wabanaki Indian nations in Maine and beyond—and it was something we should document. Costing it out and finding that it was prohibitive to our pockets and his, we submitted grant proposals to the Maine Humanities Council and the First Division Museum in Wheaton, Illinois. Both organizations agreed to help cover travel expenses. And so it was that we escorted Charles and documented his return to the World War II battle sites, where he had repeatedly displayed great selfless courage as a combat medic.

One of the most memorable parts of our journey was the time spent at Omaha Beach on France's Normandy coast, where Charles had landed with the first wave of assault troops on D-Day, 6 June 1944. There, under a barrage of fire, he pulled many wounded men out of the rising tide and dragged them to the relative shelter of a four-foot-high sand dune, where he treated them. He earned a Silver Star for extraordinary valor that day. It was his first combat experience.

Sixty-three years later, we walked silently behind Charles as he followed a winding trail down to Omaha Beach. This time, instead of a medical kit, he carried a small, leather bag of sacred items required for the traditional Penobscot spiritual ceremony he had planned. It was a modest, personal event—an old gentleman in a beaded vest, making a little fire, burning sweetgrass, sage and tobacco, and cleansing himself in the smoke in an effort to sanctify the place, honor those who had fallen and heal the pain within. The air was hauntingly still, and the fire burned slowly.

Our journey took us from Normandy to Mons (Belgium) to Aachen and Hürtgen Forest (Germany) to the Ardennes (Battle of the Bulge) and on to the rural hamlet of Auel (beyond Remagen and east of the Rhine River), where Charles was captured by German troops and taken POW; throughout our journey, Charles kept a daily journal, presented here along with a brief autobiography.

In this volume, Charles also describes a remarkable event that happened soon after our trip—being inducted as a knight in the Légion d'Honneur by French President Nicolas Sarkozy. The tribute, established by Napoleon Bonaparte in 1802, is France's highest honor, given for eminent service to the French Republic. It is an especially fitting award for Charles, not only because of his heroism in the war, but also because he is a descendant of Jean-Vincent d'Abbadie, Baron of Saint-Castin—an extraordinary French military officer and successful fur trader, who lived on the Maine coast in the seventeenth century and married the daughter of Penobscot Grand Chief Madockawando. But that is a story for Charles's return visit in Part II of this book, and one that will be included in the biography, *From Indian Island to Omaha Beach: The Story of Charles Shay, Penobscot Indian War Hero*, which we have the honor of writing.

Dr. Harald E. L. Prins, University Distinguished Prof. of Anthropology
and Bunny McBride, Adjunct Lecturer of Anthropology
Kansas State University

Preface

I have been encouraged to write this journal of my return to the battlefields of World War II. I will be traveling with Distinguished Professor Dr. Harald Prins and author/anthropologist Bunny McBride, both of Kansas State University, who will film and document this trip into the past for future reference and for future generations. I have been convinced by others that because of the rapidly diminishing number of veterans who participated in World War II, now is the time to record as much as possible from as many veterans as possible for the archives and for future reference by scholars and instructors who wish to do research and would like to have actual accounts of individuals who were there available to them. I hope this small contribution by me will be of use to future generations. I must mention that I have written this account as a personal letter to my wife, Lilli. She died on 5 September 2003, three months after arriving at our home on the Penobscot Indian Reservation, where we intended to spend the remainder of our days, after having renovated the buildings and landscaping the grounds. It may sound bizarre to some, but I felt more comfortable writing to someone who was very close to me.

Indian Island, Maine   CNS
September 2007

Acknowledgments

My sincere thanks go out to: Dr. Harald E. L. Prins, university distinguished Professor of anthropology, and his wife, Bunny McBride, author and anthropologist, both at Kansas State University; Dr. Paul H. Herbert (Col., U.S. Army, Ret.), executive director of First Division Museum at Cantigny; Eric Gillespie, director of the First Division Museum's Robert R. McCormick Research Center; Andrew Woods, research historian at the McCormick Center; to Margo Lukens, associate professor of English and director of academic programs, Foster Innovation Center, University of Maine; to Maria Girouard, director, Penobscot Nation Cultural and Historic Preservation Department; Bonnie Newsom, former director of the Cultural and Historic Preservation Department; and James Eric Francis Sr., Penobscot tribal historian; all of the Penobscot Indian Nation for their unsolicited support in all of my endeavors connected with the preservation of the history of our Penobscot Indian Nation. My special thanks go out to the people of the Penobscot Indian Nation for permitting me to represent them in many public events throughout my life. Woliwoni.

I

From Omaha Beach to the Légion d'Honneur

This is my written account of my first visit in sixty-three years to Omaha Beach in France and the retracing of the trek of the 16th Infantry Regiment from 6 June 1944 until 25 March 1945, at which time I was taken as prisoner of war by the German forces at the small village of Auel, Germany, which lies on the Sieg River, east of the city of Hennef.

LILLI SHAY

My Darling Lilli,

Tomorrow I will leave on a journey that will take me back to a point in my life that I have pushed out of my mind for over sixty-three years. I have forgotten so many things since then. I will be returning to Omaha Beach in Normandy, France, where I first set foot on the continent of Europe on 6 June 1944, now remembered as D-Day.

I have finished packing my bags, confirmed my flight, and I am ready to leave. A picture of you will accompany me as it always has, since you left me, whenever I have left home on an extended trip. I will say good night for now and write more tomorrow.

24 SEPTEMBER 2007

Up at 05:00, showered, made my breakfast and attended to last-minute details such as making certain that all windows are locked, turning down the thermostat, making my bed, and doing a general checkup to ensure all is in order. I forgot to tell you that I spent most of the day yesterday cleaning the house and putting fresh linen on the bed.

My flight, Bangor-Boston-Chicago, was uneventful. I was met at O'Hare Air Terminal in the city of Chicago by Harald and Bunny. Arrangements had been made for us to be picked by a chauffeur driving a large black limousine. It reminded me of my time as chauffeur with the Cary International Limousine Service in the city of Vienna in my younger days. However, this time I was the passenger, real classy.

I am now writing these words to you from my room in the Dairyman's House, where we have been invited to stay for the next four days by Dr. Paul Herbert, director of the First Division Museum. This house is located on a 500-acre plot of ground that has been named Cantigny after a WWI battleground in France. This was at one time a private estate belonging to a very wealthy family by the name McCormick. One of the sons from this family, Colonel Robert R. McCormick, editor and publisher of the *Chicago Tribune*, was a member of the 1st Infantry Division during WWI, and who had participated in the battle of Cantigny, a small village in France about twenty-five miles south of Amiens.

A decisive victory was won on 28 May 1918. Although it was not considered one of the great battles of WWI, it demonstrated that the Ameri-

AT THE DAIRYMAN'S HOUSE (AND BELOW)

can soldier was equal to any soldier that the European military could produce. This estate was donated to the 1st Division and now houses, among other things, the First Division Museum. It is funded by a large endowment to ensure its availability to future historians and its continued existence as an important museum of military history. It is my first evening here, and Harald, Bunny, and me have just returned from a pleasant evening at a very noble restaurant, where we had been invited by the museum's executive director, Paul Herbert. I will write more tomorrow.

25 SEPTEMBER 2007

Harald and Bunny spent the day doing research with the museum's research historian, Andrew Woods, a dedicated archivist, trying to retrace events that took place from Omaha Beach and on through many engagements with the enemy until 25 March 1945, at which time I was taken as a POW by German forces. There is so very little that I can remember from this period. Perhaps this sounds strange. However, I think one tries to forget those ex-

periences in life that are not very pleasant. You know that I never discussed my military service with you, although you were the closest person to me for almost fifty-seven years. Anyway, let us forget this for now. We spent another pleasant evening with Eric Gillespie, director of the museum's research center, who had invited the three of us out for dinner.

26 SEPTEMBER 2007

HARALD PRINS AND ANDREW WOODS

Another busy day; Harald and Bunny were still involved with research work, while I was occupied with activities involving seven other veterans from WWII, who will be relating their experiences in two live PBS television broadcasts produced by WIPB. The title of this program is *Echoes of War: Stories From the Big Red One,* and we were being instructed

WITH HARALD PRINS AND ANDREW WOODS

On the Omaha Beach set

as to what will take place; we did a test interview in preparation for the shows, which will air tomorrow, 27 September 2007, from 12:00 to 13:00 and again at 19:00 to 20:00.

This live program will be sent out to approximately twenty-five Public Television stations in ten different states across the country, with an expected audience of about twenty-eight million, and will eventually be posted on the Internet for anybody else wishing to see it. The interviews are being conducted by history professors from Ball State University, Muncie, Indiana. They are responsible for the whole affair. During the test interview, Ed Raymond, a former Navy lieutenant, had a bad fall off the Omaha Beach display set and injured his hand. I had to spring in as a medic and perform first aid on his injured hand.

With WIPB producer and WWII veteran Ed Raymond

27 SEPTEMBER 2007

Today we were up again at about 06:30 and had a leisurely breakfast. We discussed responses to questions that I would be expected to answer during the live interview. The same questions, with perhaps a little variation, will be asked both times. Not being accustomed to being interviewed publicly, it is difficult for me to appear before a camera for a live interview.

27 SEPTEMBER 2007, 21:00 HOURS

The interviews went off very nicely, and I am very happy to have it all behind me. Bunny and Harald were able to watch the interviews on TV and told me the entire broadcast went off very nicely and was very impressive. I hope to receive DVD copies of the event, enough for family and friends. Goodnight for now.

WITH FELLOW WWII VETERANS INTERVIEWED FOR PUBLIC TELEVISION.

28 September 2007

Today was again spent by Harald and Bunny doing research. I spent time trying to catch up with my diary entries. I am a bit behind. We have made friends with some of the personnel who are working in the motor pool. They have a few jeeps, half-tracks, and other equipment from WWII that are used for special occasions. Today was one of those days. There were about a hundred and fifty veterans from the Battle of the Bulge visiting the center, and these old vehicles were on display for them.

The people in charge of the display asked Harald, Bunny, and I if we would like to take a ride in one of the vehicles. We chose a half-track. It was very loud and uncomfortable to ride in, but the experience was interesting.

We had been invited out for lunch following our ride, and it was quite late when we returned to our quarters, so we spent the remainder of the evening just relaxing and talking. Harald, of course, was occupied with his

THIS PHOTO SHOWS AL POTYEN, CONSERVATION AND EXHIBITS TECHNICIAN AT THE FIRST DIVISION MUSEUM'S MILITARY VEHICLE COLLECTION, DISPLAYS AND PARADES. HE IS THE ONE WHO ARRANGED FOR US TO RIDE IN THE HALF-TRACK. HE ALSO PULLED OUT AN OLD WWII COMBAT MEDIC KIT FOR ME TO SEE.

notes and paperwork, to ensure that he is well prepared for what lies ahead of us. Another day gone, tomorrow we pack and leave for the airport, continuing on to Paris and the next phase of Project Omaha Beach. We are now beginning the most important and strenuous part of our trip. From here on everything will be recorded in interviews, video, and photos, so that a report can be compiled for future reference and also for the people who supported us with grants making it possible for this project to become a reality. This project has taken a lot of preparation, and all of the credit goes to Bunny and Harald, who have dedicated themselves to its success.

29 SEPTEMBER 2007

I am up at 06:30—showered, cleaned up my room a little bit and placed all of my things out for packing. We will be picked up and driven to the airport by a limousine service at 14:15 hours. Yesterday was also laundry day, and this morning I will do the ironing and finish packing. Bunny and I made a tour of the McCormick mansion, now a museum, while Harald went through archive papers in preparation for the next phase of Project Omaha Beach. The tour of the museum was most interesting and gave some curious information about the wife of Robert R. McCormick. She evidently was ten years older than her husband, Robert, but they kept that a secret. When she died, Robert played along with her secret and had the birth date she had chosen for herself placed on the tombstone.

The chauffeur of the limousine was a bit late picking us up, because he had been sent to the wrong building by the security guards at the gate to the estate, but he eventually found us, and after loading our luggage we were on our way to the airport. Our plane was one and a half hours late to take off, so we had time on our hands to have a small lunch and talk about our stay at Cantigny, where we had been treated with great respect and were able to make many new friends that we will not soon forget.

30 SEPTEMBER 2007

We arrived at Charles de Gaulle Airport, outside Paris, after an uneventful flight. We were met at the airport by Monsieur Frédéric Castier, who is the contact man in France for the First Division Museum. We all had coffee together and discussed our plans. Frédéric gave us some helpful in-

formation concerning our trip to Normandy. Then he drove us to the Paris railway station Saint-Lazare, where we boarded a train to continue our trip to Normandy and Omaha Beach. This was the first time that we were on our own since I had left the state of Maine one week ago. On our arrival at the small city of Bayeux in Normandy, we were not able to find a taxi and were a little bit at loss about what to do. So Harald hitched a ride into town to locate a rent-a-car office. One and a half hours later we were sit-

Our home at Le Haras de Crépon, by day (above) and by night

ting in a rented car on our way to Le Haras de Crépon, a small castle in Normandy where Harald and Bunny had booked rooms for our four-day stay, so that we could visit Omaha Beach, the American Cemetery and Memorial and other places of interest. We are the only guests at this beautiful sixteenth-century château, which is very convenient as we will not be distracted by the chatter of other people and will be better able to concentrate on the activities that lie before us.

Our gracious hostess, Pascale Landeau, prepared a five-course dinner

THE SITTING ROOM; WITH BUNNY AT BREAKFAST (ABOVE).

for us, which included a bottle of premium white wine. The label on the bottle proved it to be from stock which had won the Prize for Excellence. All of this had been planned as a welcoming ceremony for our arrival in Normandy, the most important part of our trip to Europe, and of course all was arranged again by Harald and Bunny well in advance of our departure date from the United States. This evening of superb wine and fine dining in a beautiful atmosphere of medieval furnishings, classical music, and the hospitality of Pascale and her husband Francis was an introduction as to what awaited us on our tour throughout Europe. We finally retired to our rooms for the night after a long, exhausting twenty-four hours, and I was very happy to spend a few minutes thinking of you, Lilli, before going to sleep.

1 OCTOBER 2007

After a much-needed rest following our long trip from the Cantigny estate to our new quarters at Crépon, we had a late breakfast today and then made plans to visit the beach area of Normandy. Of the utmost importance to us was our visit to Omaha Beach.

On the way there, we drove through many small villages, and my thoughts began to take me back to 6 June 1944. I began to wonder how the people of that time had been able to survive the enormous conflict that had destroyed entire villages, towns and cities. All was so different from that which I could remember. The rebuilt houses were all so neat, with flower boxes hanging in front of the windows. Cows and other animals were in the pastures. Everything looked so peaceful and serene that it was hard for me to believe that I had participated in a devastating war that had taken place here sixty-three years ago. The people, almost all from the next generation following WWII, showed no remorse and appeared to be very happy.

We surveyed some of the massive gun emplacements that had been constructed by the Germans overlooking the beaches and pointing toward the English Channel as protection in the event of an invasion. These gun emplacements had been supplemented with machinegun nests and infantrymen in the immediate beach area. It had been a concentrated and heavily defended area. As I looked out to the sea and down to the beaches, I was able to picture how vulnerable we were on that day, 6 June 1944. I could almost visualize the hundreds of ships that were standing offshore, showering these emplacements with heavy artillery and all of the other weapons they had available to them. I could imagine what was going through the mind of the German soldier when he looked out to the sea, at one of the greatest armadas that had ever been assembled in military history. Eventually he saw the thousands of Allied troops storming the beaches. He must have experienced a devastating feeling of despair, knowing that the German defenses could never hold back such an invasion.

On the other hand, the American invasion forces at Omaha Beach, who were approaching the beaches in small landing craft (each LCVP carried approximately thirty men), were thinking of survival only. The enormous firepower of both sides flying over their heads and at them, and the fear it instilled, cannot be explained in words—one has to experience such a situation to understand it. Facing a barrage of small-arms and machinegun fire, mortar shells and artillery made one begin to pray for life and survival of oneself and his comrades-in-arms.

The Germans had erected obstacles in the beach area well beyond the low tide, which prevented the landing craft from reaching the beach. Once the ramps of the landing craft went down and the order came to disembark, those men who were standing in the forefront of the landing craft were either instantly killed or severely wounded. It was every man for himself. Jumping into water up to our waists, weighed down with all sorts of gear, weapons and ammunition, plus the waterlogged clothing and boots, made it very difficult to make any progress toward the beach, dry land, and the little bit of protection offered by an embankment of sand dunes.

Seriously wounded men had no chance at all and sank to the bottom of the sea. Lightly wounded men were able to make progress toward the safety of the beaches, some by discarding all of their gear, which made them ineffective for combat. It was a miracle that any of us were able to reach the beach and the protection that the embankments provided.

The dunes were anywhere from three to six feet high—modest shelter desperately needed. Once the protection of the embankment was reached, it provided the opportunity for one to regain his senses and for the officers and noncommissioned officers to make an attempt to bring some order into a situation of total chaos. I began immediately to do that which I had been trained for: treating the wounded by bandaging wounds, applying tourniquets to stop heavy bleeding, applying makeshift splints to broken bones, administering morphine to relieve severe pain, and in general trying to make the wounded somewhat comfortable.

For reasons unknown to me, my attention was drawn to the treacherous sea and the rising tide, and it was then that I saw that so many men who had

GERMAN ARTILLERY ON THE NORMANDY COAST

been wounded were floundering in the water, trying to stay afloat. The tide was rising rapidly, and many of them were doomed to drown if nobody came to their help. My instincts took command of my thinking, and I knew that I had to help them. All of them had been wounded to some degree and were unable to help themselves. I left what I was doing and returned to the sea, which was red with the blood of the dead and wounded. I began pulling the wounded up beyond the waterline by grabbing them under their armpits. I do not know where my strength came from, but I was able to help several of the wounded to the relative safety of the beach, before I myself sank down in exhaustion.

I returned to the shelter of the embankment, and after a few minutes of rest, I resumed my efforts until I was

OUR 1ST DIVISION ASSAULT TROOPS STORMING OMAHA BEACH ON D-DAY, 6 JUNE 1944 (AND OPPOSITE PAGE)

not able to do anymore. I have no idea how many wounded men I helped that day, but numbers were not important—the important thing was that at least I was able to save some of them. One must not forget that this dilemma was repeating itself up and down the beach and that I was

operating in a very small, confined area under intense small-arms and machinegun fire. It will never be known how many wounded men drowned because they could not help themselves and no help came to them.

As the firepower of the German forces began to diminish, I was able to move more freely over a greater area. As I was walking the beach, I came upon a fellow combat medic, Pvt. Edward Morozewicz, who had a serious stomach wound. I knew that he was slowly dying. He was conscious enough to know who I was, and we greeted each other. I bandaged his wounds as best I could and administered a shot of

morphine to relieve his pain. I knew there was no help for him. I said goodbye to him and we parted—forever.

I remained on the beach until late afternoon on that day. In the chaos and confusion that came after the initial landing on the shores of Omaha Beach, I had

become separated from my unit. I eventually followed other foot soldiers up a draw that led inland from the beach, seeing many dead American and German soldiers on the way. I was able to reconnect with the medical detachment to which I belonged. Following the regrouping of what was left of the 16th Infantry Regiment, I was able to return to what was left of F Company, to which I had been assigned before the invasion.

God was with those who survived that infamous day. I attribute my survival to the prayers and power of my mother, and I know that she is still watching over me today.

2 OCTOBER 2007

We visited the beaches of Normandy, trying to revive my memory of what took place, over sixty-three years ago. It was not easy, but when one thinks of the time lapsed and my age, eighty-three, it is understandable. The day went by on us very fast. It was midafternoon by the time we made our intended visit to the Normandy American Cemetery and Memorial, which sits on the hills above Omaha Beach. We did not arrive there until about 15:15 or 15:30.

DAMAGED COLLEVILLE-SUR-MER CHURCH

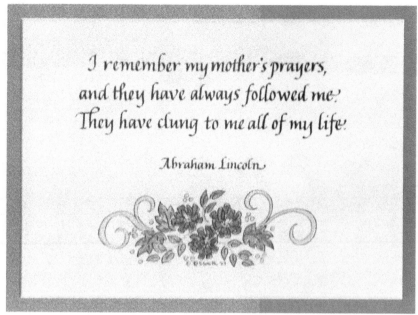

I remember my mother's prayers,
and they have always followed me.
They have clung to me all of my life.

Abraham Lincoln

The words of Abraham Lincoln in calligraphic design given to me
by the artist Sharon Smith of Muncie, Indiana.

As we approached the information desk and introduced ourselves, I was immediately greeted by my name as if they had been waiting for us. We later found out that the cemetery administrators had already been informed of our coming by Frédéric Castier, the gentleman who had greeted us on our arrival in Paris at Charles de Gaulle Airport. We were introduced to the superintendent of the cemetery and members of his staff. They all treated us with great respect. During our talk with the staff, I was informed that I would be participating in the flag-lowering ceremony that was to take place at 16:00 hours.

My participation in this ceremony was completely unexpected and unplanned, and this is the reason I mention our time of arrival as only a few minutes before the ceremony was to take place. It appears that the spirits of the dead comrades-in-arms were directing us to be there at this particular time. The ceremony was emotionally very moving, and I was greatly honored to be able to participate.

After the flag-lowering, I visited the grave site of Private Edward Morozewicz, paying my respects to a hero. He was a recipient of the Silver Star, awarded after his death, for valor shown on 6 June 1944. He had paid the ultimate price, while performing his duties as a combat medic on Omaha Beach.

At the grave of Edward Morozewicz, Normandy American Cemetery.

We learned that there are approximately 9,380 brave soldiers buried here. The Star of David identifies Jewish grave sites, and white crosses for all others.

Flag-lowering ceremony at Normandy American Cemetery and Memorial

It had been a very long day for us again, and we had dinner before returning to our quarters. We spent a little time visiting and talking with our hosts before finally retiring for the evening.

1ST DIVISION AT OMAHA BEACH

3 OCTOBER 2007

Today, before visiting another museum and performing a traditional Native American ceremony on the beach of Normandy, we stopped by the offices of our host, so that Harald and Bunny could read received e-mails on the office computers and also send out replies.

The first museum we visited was a small, private museum operated by twenty-nine-year-old Pierre-Louis Gosselin. He became interested in WWII history at the age of nine. Over the years he has collected all sorts of items connected with D-Day. He named his museum the Big Red One Assault Museum to honor the 1st Infantry Division. He has a large collection of various pieces of military equipment, uniforms, and weapons. In addition, he has assembled albums with pictures and accounts of combat experiences written by veteran soldiers who have visited his museum. Taking into consideration that this is a one-man museum, he has many valuable items and information, and he has much knowledge of events that took place on 6 June 1944.

After leaving the Assault Museum, we went to a small restaurant and had lunch—it was not very good. Our next goal was Omaha Beach, where

I was to perform a Native American ceremony for fallen comrades and my ancestors.

The weather at this time was not exceptionally nice—cloudy and gray with a light wind prevailing, not at all ideal for performing my ceremony on the beaches. We drove to a parking area of the Normandy American Cemetery and proceeded to pass through the security checkpoint of the complex. I was carrying a bag which contained all of the items I needed for the ceremony, and as the staff of the checkpoint already knew that I was returning to perform a ceremony, we were permitted to pass without having our bags checked. We proceeded on a path that led from the cemetery area down to the beaches, and suddenly the cloud cover began to clear. When we reached the beach, the sun was shining, and the breeze had quieted. I interpreted this as another sign that the spirits were again watching over us.

After locating the approximate area where I had once sought cover and treated the wounded on that infamous day, I began preparing for the ceremony there. I made a fire using paper and kindling wood that I had obtained from our hosts at Crépon. Once the fire was burning, I deposited sage into the flames and smudged myself with the smoke from this fire, to

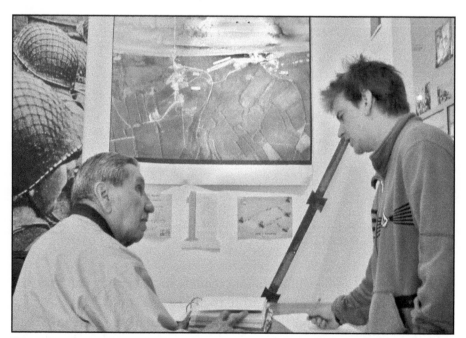

WITH PIERRE-LOUIS GOSSELIN, OWNER OF THE BIG RED ONE ASSAULT MUSEUM, COLLEVILLE-SUR-MER, FRANCE.

HONORING THE FALLEN IN A PENOBSCOT INDIAN CEREMONY AT OMAHA BEACH

cleanse my mind and my body, before sending my message to all who had participated in Operation Overlord sixty-three years ago.

I then concentrated on those men who, by sacrificing their lives, had paid the ultimate price. I took tobacco from a pouch I had with me, touching it to my forehead, saying a prayer, and then dropping it into the

fire. I repeated this process to all four directions, East, South, West, and North. At the same time, I was remembering my ancestors, my brothers and sisters—and not to forget you, Lilli, my wife and companion for fifty-seven years. I then burned sweetgrass, going through the same ritual of the four directions and remembering the dead with a prayer. I closed the

ceremony by covering the fire with sand, as it had served its purpose. I did not want to go away and leave it burning.

As I was performing the ceremony, the thought went through my mind that I would soon be joining all of them, and I was consoled knowing that all would be there to greet me when I arrived. (The 23rd Psalm promises: "The Lord is my shepherd; I shall not want." He will lead me to the Spiritual World, where comrades, friends, ancestors, family, and my wife will be waiting for me, and they in turn will lead me into their realm.)

After another long, exhausting and emotional day, we returned to Crépon to spend time with our hosts, Pascale and François. This was our last evening together. We shared a bottle of champagne, which I purchased yesterday for this occasion, and discussed our experiences of the last four days. We had a very enjoyable evening just talking and getting better acquainted. I think champagne tends to loosen the tongue.

4 OCTOBER 2007

Today we prepared to move onto the next phase of Project Omaha Beach. Harald and Bunny had made arrangements for our train ride from Caen to Paris and then on to Mons, Belgium, where we would spend the next two days with Harald's sister and her husband. I will also be meeting Harald's mother for the first time. She has traveled from her home in the Netherlands for this family meeting.

When we left our quarters in Crépon, we had a very tight schedule. Our train was departing Caen at 12:10, so we had only two hours to load our luggage, drive in half an hour to the city of Caen, turn in our rental car, find the train station, buy our tickets, and board the train. Ten minutes after we boarded, the train left the station, and we were on our way to Mons, with a couple of changes in between.

On our arrival at the Mons station, we were met by Joris Diepen, Harald's brother-in-law, and after a forty-five-minute drive we arrived at his chalet, a very large house in the countryside, complete with three friendly dogs, two cats, five peacocks, and chickens. Here I met Harald's mother, Ita Prins-Poorter, and his sister Jerrie, who is Joris' wife. The reception and greetings were very sincere, and I was accepted into the family. Shortly after arriving, we sat in the garden over a glass of good wine, to talk and become better acquainted with each other. Joris and

Jerrie prepared a welcome dinner for us, which also included a glass of the best wine. After spending a very pleasant evening together, we retired to our rooms for a much-needed rest.

WITH PASCALE AND FRANÇOIS, PROPRIETORS OF LE HARAS DE CRÉPON.

ITA PRINS-POORTER AND ME

5 OCTOBER 2007

Today, breakfast at 08:30, and plans were made to visit areas of the Belgian-French border where the 1st Infantry Division was engaged with the German Forces during WWII. After driving several miles (six of us in two cars—I with Joris in his black Porsche), we decided to stop at a restaurant on the way, because Joris told us that there were not very many restaurants located in the area we were traveling to. The restaurant was Rancho Grill, an interesting name for a restaurant located in the Belgian-French border area.

A five-foot Indian figure carved out of wood stood at the entrance, and inside we saw several more. As we looked around the rooms, we saw that the walls were covered with authentic pictures of Buffalo Bill Cody and many, many photos of Indians from that era. Of course, this was the cue for Harald to locate the proprietor and to introduce me as a Penobscot Indian from the state of Maine and to tell her what our mission was for being in this particular area. The lady ended up inviting us for a round of drinks and paying for our dessert. On leaving the restaurant, she introduced all of us to her husband, and the goodbyes were full of enthusiasm. I told her that I would send pictures of Penobscot Indians and asked if she would add them to her collection.

We then continued on our mission and found some areas where the two regiments—mine the 16th and Melvin Neptune's the 26th—had engaged the enemy, resulting in heavy losses for the German forces, but there was

WITH WOODEN INDIAN AND LÉA CAZEAUX

WITH JORIS DIEPEN

not much to see that could remind me that I had once passed through here. After another long day, we returned home to spend another pleasant evening with the family members of Harald.

6 OCTOBER 2007

Today we were a bit undecided as to what we should undertake. We had two choices. One was to visit Bütgenbach in the Belgian Ardennes and spend the day visiting old battle sites again. This, however, did not sound very promising, because one does not see very much. There are really no battle sites to see anymore, we were told, as everything has been rebuilt.

Our second choice was to drive to the city of Mons to meet with a man we did not know but who had told Harald over the telephone that he had some interesting information to share with us. We had heard about him from a woman we met yesterday—an acquaintance of Joris and Jerrie's. Not knowing what was in store for us, we chose to meet with the unknown man. After some delay, we finally left home in two cars to a rendezvous point on the road leading to Mons.

This first meeting was very emotional. The man, Philippe Huberland, who is about forty-five years old, told us a story about his father who had been a prisoner of the German army and had been freed by the American army. As he told his story he had tears in his eyes, saying that he was ever thankful that the Americans had freed his father and that they had given his country (Belgium) back its freedom. By this time he had me in tears also, and he just kept placing his arms around me and repeating his thankfulness for what the Americans had done for his country. This was a sort of emotional enthusiasm that I had never experienced before this meeting. The woman we met yesterday and who put us in contact with Philippe was also there and full of the same thankfulness and enthusiasm. One must remember that all of this is taking place on an open road sixty-three years after the fact.

Eventually, we all boarded our cars, and our newfound friend Philippe directed us to the home of his friend Jean-Louis Claessens. Once there, we were again greeted with much enthusiasm by Jean-Louis and his family. He took us through his house to the back yard and a small garage, where he showed us his pride and joy, an old U.S. Army personnel carrier.

I thought it was a one-ton truck, but Jean-Louis called it a 6X6, and I am sure he knew what he was talking about because this was his hobby. Anyway, this vehicle was in perfect condition. He had spent six years working on it to bring it back into tiptop condition. It still had all of the original ID and insignia numbers on the front and rear bumpers, and the

COLLECTORS OF OLD U.S. ARMY VEHICLES IN MONS

WITH PHILIPPE, JEAN-LOUIS, AND BUNNY.

white star that identified military vehicles in those old days was painted on the hood.

Jean-Louis jumped into the driver's seat, and the 6x6 started immediately. Due to high fuel prices, the engine had been converted to run on liquid gas. He pulled the truck out of the garage to take us on a ride. But before we left, he went into the house and returned with two period army officer's jackets, one for himself and one for me. Both jackets were practically new. His was complete with insignias and name patch. Mine, although without any insignia, was a perfect fit.

We all loaded up—I in the front with Jean-Louis and the rest of the crew in the rear. Jean-Louis then drove us to another friend; the greetings repeated themselves, and again we were conducted into a garage and shown old army vehicles and equipment, all in perfect condition and running order.

In addition to his Jeep and trucks, this man had an old Harley-Davidson motorcycle. Complete with U.S. Navy insignia, it dated back to the year 1940—a true rarity.

Beer and wine were brought out, and we sat down to talk. We were told that there are over one hundred collectors in Mons, with well over

WITH JEAN-LOUIS—I AM WEARING A WWII OFFICER'S COAT.

one hundred U.S. Army vehicles of all types and all in perfect condition. Once a year, in August, the city celebrates its 1944 liberation from German occupying forces, and all of this equipment participates in a Tanks in Town parade. I was invited to attend the 6 June 2009 celebration of the 65th Anniversary of D-Day. Collectors from all of Europe will drive their antique U.S. military vehicles to Normandy to participate in this great event. The new friends that I have made in Mons, Belgium, hope to meet me there.

We again loaded onto our 6x6, and I thought we were returning to the home of Jean-Louis. Instead, we were driven to a large fenced-in area, where we saw a tarp-covered Sherman tank parked outside of the city garage. This was supposedly the first U.S. Army tank to enter the city of Mons when it was liberated by American forces. The story was told as follows.

When the U.S. Army rolled into the city with their tanks in the fall of 1944, one of the citizens wrote down the numbers of the leading tank, and a few years after the war the city government contacted U.S. Army headquarters and related this incident. U.S. Army authorities conducted

AUTHOR ON SHERMAN TANK

a search and were able to locate this tank and they, in turn, had the tank shipped to Belgium, and it was presented to the city of Mons as a gift of the U.S. Army.

Next, someone arrived with keys to the garage and opened the doors. Inside we were able to view two tanks, both in perfect condition, one a Sherman tank with a small gun, perhaps 75 mm, and next to it a German Tiger tank with an 88 mm artillery piece. The Sherman tank was dwarfed by the Tiger tank and proved that the German army was, in my mind, much more advanced in military technology than the Americans at that particular time in history.

Harald then made me aware that two of the men were pouring gas from a container into the Sherman tank. They then started the motor and drove it out of the garage. I was invited to mount the tank into the upper hatch and was taken for a ride around the grounds for about twenty minutes. This was a complete and unexpected experience for me.

Following my tank ride, I was presented with two caps, one blue and one green, with the insignia TANKS IN TOWN embroidered on the front. After the tank had been garaged again, we were all invited by the tank captain to share a drink with the tank crew in a nearby bar and restaurant.

TANK CREW, AUTHOR AT CENTER BACK ROW.

I was asked to autograph the caps of all the crew and in turn asked for signatures from all of the crew in one of the caps given to me. It is difficult for me to describe the enthusiasm that I found throughout my tour of Belgium. I especially remember one of the crew members, a seventeen-year-old boy, who was so impressed that I was an American Indian and a WWII veteran. (He is pictured here, wearing coveralls.) One must remember that this young man is perhaps the third generation of those people that experienced WWII. Here, even these young people are grateful for what took place sixty-three years ago.

We said a tearful goodbye to our newfound friends and returned to the home of our hosts. Because it was our last day and evening with them, they had invited all of us out for dinner—fine dining, fine wine, and good conversation. This was a goodbye celebration, because tomorrow we are leaving for Brussels to take the train to Luxembourg City.

7 OCTOBER 2007

We arrived in Luxembourg City on schedule and were met at the train station by His Excellency Carlo Krieger, Luxembourg's ambassador to China and very close friend of Harald. Having offered to host and guide us during our stay, Carlo showed us to our hotel (Golden Tulip Hotel Central Molitor), within walking distance of the station. We deposited our luggage, freshened up a bit, and were on our way for a small tour of the city.

The weather was beautiful, so we were able to sit outside at a park restaurant and enjoy a dance performance by a Romanian group dressed in the traditional costumes of their country. After resting and enjoying the show, we went by taxi to the Luxembourg American Cemetery and Memorial in a beautiful wooded area in Hamm, just three miles east of downtown Luxembourg. At the entrance to this complex, we were met by the cemetery's superintendent, who asked us to register and then provided us with brochures and historical information, telling us that the remains

WITH HIS EXCELLENCY CARLO KRIEGER, LUXEMBOURG AMBASSADOR TO CHINA (LEFT), AND THE DIRECTOR OF THE LUXEMBOURG AMERICAN CEMETERY AND MEMORIAL.

of 5,000 American soldiers were buried here, including General George S. Patton Jr. Looking at the inscriptions on the grave markers, we were able to identify the grave sites of Native Americans and also a few gravesites of men from the state of Maine.

We spent about one and one half hours visiting the cemetery. The superintendent then asked me if I would assist with the flag-lowering ceremony. Of course I agreed immediately, as this was a great and unexpected honor for me. After paying our respects to the soldiers who had lost their lives in the Battle of the Bulge in the Ardennes, we were the last people to leave the cemetery. We returned to our hotel for a short rest and a change of clothing.

Our host had invited us out for dinner that evening, and we were joined by people who represented may different countries. There was His Excellency Carlo Krieger, on leave from his post for a week; a former assistant minister of Carlo's, who was now working in the Ministry of Foreign Affairs; a young lady who came from Moscow; a young man from Luxembourg, whose wife was from Kazakhstan; she performed in the theater and was also an exotic dancer; Dr. Harald E. L. Prins, distinguished professor of anthropology at Kansas State University; Bunny McBride, anthropologist and author at Kansas State University; and yours truly, Charles Norman Shay, elder of the Penobscot Indian Nation and veteran of WWII.

We said our goodbyes to all tonight, because tomorrow morning we are leaving by train to Aachen, Germany, and then on to the town of Remagen on the Rhine River, other areas where the 16th Infantry Regiment participated in many bloody battles.

8 OCTOBER 2007

We arrived in Aachen in about six hours. We had stopped over at Clervaux, a small Ardennes village, where we wanted to visit a museum which was housed in an old castle. Unfortunately, it was closed on Mondays, so we boarded the next train and continued on to Liège, Belgium, where we changed trains for the final trip to Aachen.

We found modest lodging at Hotel Danmark near the Aachen train

DINNER THAT EVENING

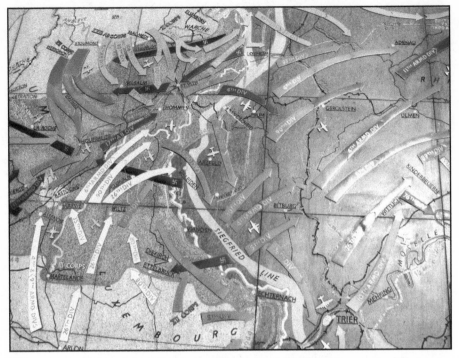

THIS STONE MAP AT THE LUXEMBOURG AMERICAN CEMETERY AND MEMORIAL
SHOWS THE 1ST DIVISION AND FELLOW ALLIED DIVISIONS IN THE BATTLE OF THE
BULGE AND BREAKING THROUGH THE SIEGFRIED LINE.

station. We explored the city on foot, and the next day rented a car to visit
surrounding areas of interest that had to do with the fall of the city to
American forces.

It was in Aachen that the 26th Infantry Regiment fought house-to-
house battles until the city capitulated. The plan was for the 18th Infantry
to approach the city from the west and isolate it from that direction. The
26th Infantry was to attack from the south and enter the city. The 16th
Infantry was to penetrate the Scharnhorst Line, seize high ground on
the east side of the city, and swing northeast and occupy the town of
Eilendorf. After over one month of fierce fighting for the city of Aachen,
the commanding officer of the German forces finally surrendered the city
on 21 October 1944 to the men of the 26th.

Melvin Neptune was a member of the 26th Inf. Reg. and had lived
through this fierce battle for the city of Aachen. Although we had been
very near each other throughout the European campaign, we did not see
each other in Europe after our first encounter on the ship that had carried

From left, back: The first sergeant, Lieutenant Otsby, Lieutenant Jankowski; Private Shay (left) and the radio man, outside Aachen, Germany.

us to the Continent. Our next meeting took place on our small Indian reservation after the war had ended.

Today, touring the outskirts of Aachen, we visited the church in the town of Eilendorf. There we encountered a man on the street and engaged him in conversation. This man was born in 1937 and therefore was seven years old when I was in the area with the 16th Inf. Regt., in the fall of 1944. He told us that he remembered the bombing, shelling, and fighting that took place in this small village at that time. He related an incident that he recalled; he and his family and some others had taken refuge in the cellar of a house that was then hit by a bomb, causing it to collapse. Some members of the group were buried alive. Others were able to extricate themselves and began to dig frantically with bare hands, looking for other survivors. One dead child and two dead adults were pulled from the rubble. He also told us that one of the streets in this small village carried the name of one of the German generals, an aristocrat with the title of *Graf* (count), from WWII. However, this same man had given the order for the killing of some children who had been caught stealing food, which they needed to stay alive. This incident was not uncovered until many years after the war had ended. Of course, the necessary action was immediately taken to rename the street.

RETURNING TO HÜRTGEN FOREST, I SAW THE OLD CASTLE OF MÉRODE (OPPOSITE),
WHERE MELVIN NEPTUNE FOUGHT.

We also visited Hamich and several castles in the area where the 1st
Inf. Div. had fought many battles. One of these battles took place in the
woods between Mérode and Laufenburg and was a victory for the German
forces when two companies of the 26th Inf. Regt., C and E Company,
were almost annihilated at Mérode. Melvin was a member of E Company
but lived to tell his story.

10–12 OCTOBER 2007

We left Aachen in our rented car and proceeded to the village of
Lannesdorf, where we were able to board a ferry that carried us across
the Rhine River to Königswinter. From there we continued northeastward
from the Rhine for about an hour to the village of Oberpleis, our home
base for the next three days. We visited numerous small villages where
various battles had taken place. It was, however, difficult for me to make
a connection between the villages of today and when I saw them almost
sixty-four years ago.

The weather was beautiful on our first day here. We drove through the countryside on our way to Erpel on the east side of the Rhine. The Ludendorff Bridge once proudly spanned from here to Remagen on the opposite side of the river. In March of 1945, this railroad bridge was taken intact by the 9th Armored Division, but afterwards it collapsed due to the impact of German rocket fire, when the Germans tried to stop the Americans from sending across reinforcements for the bridgehead that had been established on the river's east shore. There was never a direct hit to the bridge with these rockets, but the explosive power of the shells landing nearby caused the bridge to collapse. The massive stone and cement abutments of this once-imposing structure still stand on both sides of the river and present a very impressive view.

Sitting on the second floor of Zur Brücke restaurant on the east shore, we had a beautiful view of the Rhine River and Remagen on the opposite shore. While enjoying the view, we ordered drinks and a cheese plate with bread and enjoyed ourselves even more.

On our last day in the Rhine Valley, we drove northeast to Hennef, which lies on the south

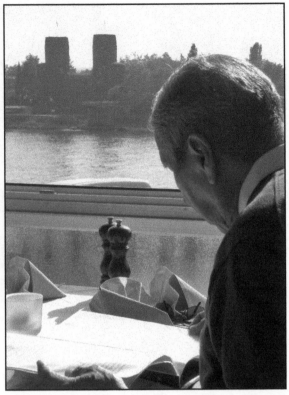

At Restaurant Zur Brücke, overlooking the Rhine River and Remagen.

bank of the Sieg River. It was in this area that fighting became very intense in late March 1945, when the 1st Army launched its long-awaited offensive. Harald's research, combined with my memories, indicates that this is where the infantry squad that I was attached to as a medic was sent on a reconnaissance mission, crossing a railroad bridge over the Sieg River into the village of Auel, Germany. Here, the squad ran

THE OLD ABUTMENTS OF THE BRIDGE AT REMAGEN ARE VISIBLE ACROSS THE RHINE.

into a German Tiger tank backed up by infantry, and the war came to an end for me, as I was taken as a POW. Today, when we visited Auel, the weather was dull and cloudy—the perfect setting for revisiting one of the darkest days of my life. Perhaps the spirits were at work again.

THE VILLAGE OF AUEL, WHERE I WAS CAPTURED IN 1945.

The railroad bridge still extends over the Sieg River that winds along the village, and the place still has a rural feel to it, with cattle in the pastures behind the old farmhouses and barns. But the buildings have been renovated, the yards landscaped, and the streets paved, so the general appearance seemed so different from that which I could remember.

We returned to our hotel in Oberpleis for a short rest and then went to a very nice restaurant for dinner. Our waitress was from France and spoke English and was most interested in the purpose of our visit in this particular area. We visited the same restaurant the next evening, and I gave her copies which I had been carrying with me of the brochure of my teepee.

With this visit to the site of my capture in Auel, we have now completed Project Omaha Beach. We celebrated the successful completion of our work by going to another fine restaurant, one that we had not visited before. Tomorrow we pack our bags again and prepare to return to Paris, where we will remain for three days and then return to the United States, and I to my home on the Indian reservation.

13 OCTOBER 2007

Today we were ready to leave very early, loaded our luggage into our rented car, had breakfast, and departed our hotel in Oberpleis 06:50 hours. Timing was very important, because we had a two-hour ride to Aachen, where we had to return our rental car and purchase tickets for our train to Paris, scheduled to leave the station at 11:00. I was dropped of at the train station with the luggage, and Bunny and Harald left to return the rented car.

Upon their return, we purchased our train tickets, but by that time

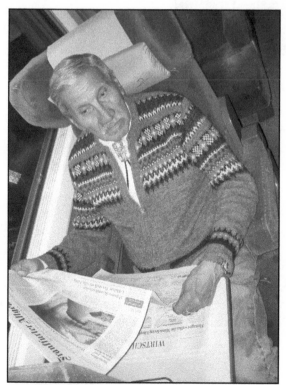

only first-class tickets were available. I think the spirits had intervened again, because on our last train trip in Europe we were traveling in style. We had time for coffee and pastries at the station, before our train departed on schedule.

We traveled via Liège and Brussels at over 200 miles an hour. This was a very fast luxury train. Looking out of the window, I saw we were traveling parallel to the *Autobahn*. Automobiles looked as if they were moving very slowly, but were probably clocking 100 miles an hour or more.

READING THE *FRANKFURTER ALLGEMEINE* IN THE HIGH-SPEED TRAIN TO PARIS

Our train fare covered lunch and drinks, including wine or beer. I have done a lot of international traveling in my life, and when one travels by air today all of these luxuries have been done away with. On long flights, one may receive a meal with water or coffee, but wine and beer will cost at least $5.00.

On arriving in Paris, there seemed to have been a shortage of taxis, because we had to stand in a long line for approximately forty-five minutes before we were finally able to have a taxi that delivered us to Hôtel du Brésil near the Luxemburg Gardens. The rooms were very small. Mine had a bathroom that measured about two by nine feet and contained a toilet, wash bowl, and shower. This was definitely not a bathroom for a fat man. Sigmund Freud was also a guest at this hotel in the year of 1885. We may have occupied the same room, who knows?

After dropping off our luggage and freshening up a bit, we took our first walk in the city of Paris, taking in its beauty, including the Luxembourg Gardens near our hotel. About half an hour after leaving our hotel we came to the magnificent Notre Dame Cathedral. We were fortunate in that we arrived there just in time to witness a multimedia presentation inside the cathedral. This presentation was most interesting and informative. We learned about the construction of the cathedral and about damage that had been inflicted during wars through its history and other things about the cathedral that one is not normally aware of.

Following this presentation at Notre Dame Cathedral, we decided to go for dinner. However, the Rugby World Cup playoff was taking place this evening at the Stade de France and was being broadcast on big-screen televisions in practically every café and restaurant. This was too much for me after another long day, so I decided to return to the hotel where I had a small bottle of wine and some cookies. Harald and Bunny escorted me back to the hotel and then went out to dinner without me at the café nearest our hotel.

14 October 2007

Today we had a late and leisurely breakfast. Project Omaha Beach was behind us, and we still had two days in Paris to enjoy ourselves. We walked

through the Luxembourg Gardens again. Harald had an appointment with some people at UNESCO (United Nations Educational, Scientific and Cultural Organization), which has its headquarters in Paris. So, therefore, Bunny and I decided to visit the Eiffel Tower and meet with Harald at UNESCO later that afternoon. The line was so long that it appeared we

AT NOTRE DAME DE PARIS

wouldn't be able to go up the tower and still make it to UNESCO at the appointed time. After waiting nearly forty-five minutes, Bunny approached the guards and said she was with an eighty-three-year-old American Indian who was a WWII veteran who had been part of the forces that stormed Omaha Beach on D-Day. She explained that the Eiffel Tower was the main

AT THE EIFFEL TOWER

Lunch with our host, Jens Boel, chief archivist, UNESCO.

With Jens Boel outside UNESCO

WITH MY OLD FRIEND MAHMOUD GHANDER

site I wanted to see in Paris. Then, for good measure, she mentioned that I had been nominated for the Légion d'honneur. Apparently that did the trick, for we were invited to go to the front of the line, making it to the top of the tower, despite our tight schedule.

Following our visit to the Eiffel Tower, Bunny and I took a taxi to UNESCO and met Harald and his Danish friend, Jens Boel, UNESCO's chief archivist. As none of us had had lunch, we were invited by Jens to a small restaurant. Later he invited us to his office in the UNESCO building, and I was introduced to one of his coworkers, whom I already knew from when we worked together at the International Atomic Energy Agency (IAEA) in the city of Vienna, Austria, in the year of 1978-79. It was my old friend Mahmoud Ghander, an Egyptian citizen. We had both worked in the same department in Vienna, and he later left and traveled to Paris, where he was able to gain employment. He was to retire shortly after our meeting.

Leaving UNESCO, we walked to a famous historic site—Napoleon Bonaparte's tomb, located under the dome of the Hôtel des Invalides, a building constructed in the late seventeenth century to house aging veterans. However, because we had not checked on the opening and closing hours, we arrived too late and were not able to gain admittance.

L'Hôtel national des Invalides

This was unfortunate, because I would have liked very much to have seen it. Harald began a filmed interview of me in this historic setting, but the day had become cold and misty, and I was tired, so we discontinued the interview. We took a taxi back to our hotel for a rest, before going to a nearby restaurant for dinner.

SITTING BY FOUNTAINS AT THE LOUVRE

15 OCTOBER 2007

This was our last day in Paris. As there are many historical places and buildings to see in this beautiful city, three days is just not enough time. The weather was beautiful. After our usual French breakfast of juice, coffee, and French bread with jam, we spent the day just wandering about—walking along the Seine River, enjoying the courtyards of the Louvre Museum, and strolling through the Tuileries Garden to the Place de la Concorde. We sat in the sun by a fountain and had ice-cream cones. We visited a church and lit candles for our ancestors and stopped at a café.

We returned to our hotel for a short rest and to freshen up a bit before going out for dinner at the Perraudin Restaurant to celebrate our last night in Paris and complete closure of Project Omaha Beach.

WITH BUNNY AND HARALD (BEHIND CAMERA) ON OUR LAST EVENING IN PARIS

Tomorrow we leave for the air terminal and return to the Untied States, after a strenuous two weeks of traveling in Europe—on top of four days at Cantigny.

16 OCTOBER 2007

Today we packed our bags for the last time. Because the Métro (subway) was within walking distance of our hotel, we decided to use this mode of transportation to the airport. It was much cheaper and very convenient for us. My flight was scheduled to leave at 13:30, with ar-

rival time in Bangor at 20:20 (including a four-hour layover in Boston). Harald and Bunny were to leave one hour later. They would fly to Chicago and then on to Kansas City. They accompanied me to my gate, and we said goodbye to each other. My flights were uneventful, and I was met at the Bangor airport by my neighbor Matthew and his brother Jim Sappier. I have finally returned to my home, after almost three weeks. I am very tired and happy to be home again. I will now spend a few days just relaxing and recovering from my trip into the past.

17 OCTOBER 2007

Today, my first full day at home, I received a telephone call at about 11:00 a.m. On the phone was Ms. Noëlle Visani, assistant to the consul general of France in Boston. She informed me that I had been selected for induction into the Légion d'honneur as *chevalier* and that she would forward more explicit instructions as soon as all arrangements for this ceremony had been completed. I was completely overwhelmed upon receiving this news and did not know what I should do next. I did know, however, that Harald had mentioned to me shortly before the end of Project Omaha Beach that he had recommended me for this great honor. But because we had been traveling for the past three weeks and we could not be contacted, he did not know the status of his recommendation. I was therefore obligated to inform Harald and Bunny immediately and pass on the good news. I also knew that what I thought would be a few days of recovery from our trip to Europe now could be forgotten. What I was about to experience over the next three weeks was beyond all my expectations, and there would be no rest for me until all was over.

A few days later, I received written confirmation. Being a member of VFW Post 3381, the Old Town Chapter, which had acted as sponsor (without obligation) of my revisit to Omaha Beach and other battle sites of WWII, I felt obligated to inform the administration about what was taking place. I talked with John Trembley, who is in charge of the administration and assistant to Post Commander Bruce Arnold. He asked me if I had any objection to his notifying Ms. Greta Sproul, one of the editors for the *Penobscot Times*. My first interview took place shortly thereafter, and from that day on my telephone never stopped ringing.

Ms. Visani informed me of all of the details connected with the award ceremony. It was to take place at the residence of the French ambassador to the United States in Washington, DC on 6 November 2007 and was to be hosted by His Excellency Nicolas Sarkozy, president of the Republic of France and grand master of the Ordre National de la Légion d'honneur on his first official visit to the United States.

This was a great honor for me, to be one of seven selected veterans of WWII. It is very seldom that one is honored, first to be selected as a recipient of this medal and secondly to have it pinned on one's tunic by such a distinguished person. It was and will remain the pinnacle of my life. This was an event that will remain in my memories for the rest of my life. I will always be extremely thankful to Prof. Dr. Harald Prins and Bunny McBride, both of whom had made all of this become a reality.

Ms. Noëlle Visani informed me that I would be escorted from my home on the Penobscot Indian Reservation to Washington, DC by the Honorable François Gauthier, consul general of France in Boston. I was also informed that I could select one person to accompany me, at their expense, and I selected James Sappier, former chief and now council member of our Penobscot Tribal Government. In addition to this, I was permitted to invite eight persons to attend the ceremony, which was to be held at the residence of the French ambassador on 6 November 2007. My choice was my son, my grandson, Harald Prins, Bunny McBride, Penobscot Chief Kirk Francis, James Sappier, Teresa Sappier, and two close friends of Harald's.

5 NOVEMBER 2007

From 18 October 2007 until today my telephone has not stopped ringing. I was called by several newspapers requesting interviews. Some were from local newspapers, others were out of state, some were over the Internet, and one was conducted over telephone lines through the Maine Public Broadcasting Network in Bangor, when I was connected to a reporter working for the BBC out of the Boston office. It was a very hectic two-and-one-half weeks.

On Monday 5 November, I was up and about very early to prepare for the arrival of the Honorable François Gauthier and his staff, who were driving from Boston and expected to arrive at approximately 11:00 hours. The plan was for Monsieur Gauthier and his staff to spend approximately

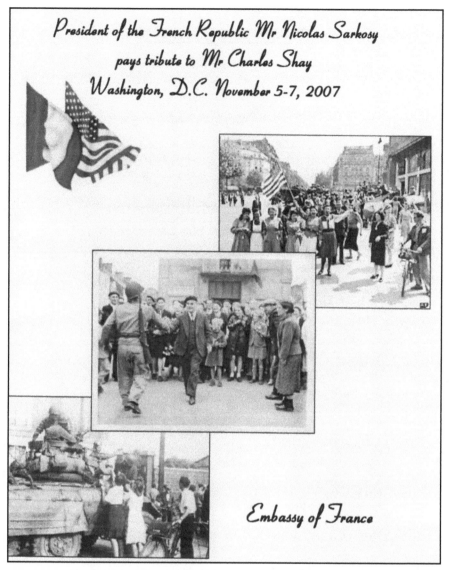

President of the French Republic Mr Nicolas Sarkosy
pays tribute to Mr Charles Shay
Washington, D.C. November 5-7, 2007

Embassy of France

ANNOUNCEMENT OF FRENCH TRIBUTE TO CHARLES SHAY

an hour at my residence and then to proceed to the Community Building to meet with the Penobscot chief, sub chief, members of the chief's council, and a few other people and family members who had been invited to attend a welcome ceremony for Monsieur Gauthier.

In my innocence I had prepared a coffee table with the thought in mind that we would be sitting down and talk over a cup of coffee before leaving for the community center. I was very wrong. At about 09:00 people

SCHEDULE OF EVENTS

Monday, November 5, 2007

18h50   Mr. Charles Shay, Mr. James Sappier, Mr. George Thompson and Mrs. Thompson arrive Reagan National Airport – Flight DL # 5675

Welcome and escort: Sergeant Major Alain Bordedebat– Cell 202-957-5852

Transfer to Park Hyatt Hotel– 24th & M Streets, NW
Tel (202) 419-6686

Nota: Check-in with personal credit card. Room and continental breakfast paid for by French Embassy

Evening at leisure

Tuesday, November 6, 2007

14h15   Pick up at Park Hyatt Hotel (lobby) by French Embassy representative and transfer to French Ambassador's residence
Escort: Sergeant Major Alain Bordedebat

14h45   Arrival at French Ambassador's Residence – 2221 Kalorama Road, NW

Welcome by WO Dany Herbert-Schinzel

15h45 – 16h15   Legion of Honor award ceremony presided over by Mr. Nicolas Sarkozy, President of the French Republic.

16h15 – 17h15   Cocktail reception

17h30   Transfer to Hotel Park Hyatt

Evening at leisure

SCHEDULE OF EVENTS (AND OPPOSITE) IN WHICH CHARLES SHAY WAS INDUCTED AS CHEVALIER (KNIGHT) DE LA LÉGION D'HONNEUR.

from the press started arriving, and before I knew what was going on, I had a house full of reporters with camera people and some people from the reservation who were also taking notes and recording what was taking place before the arrival of François Gauthier and his staff.

Wednesday, November 7, 2007

08h45   Pick-up in the hotel lobby (with luggage) after check-out
Escort: Sergeant Major Martial Payen   Cell : 202-957-8454
<u>Nota</u>: Legion of Honor recipient must wear his medal on visit to Capitol

09h45   Arrival at the U.S. Capitol

Welcome by the Honorable Nancy Pelosi, Speaker of the House
Group photograph

11h00   Address delivered by Mr. Nicolas Sarkozy, President of the French
Republic

12h30   Lunch at the French Embassy restaurant « Le Diplomate »

<u>US Veterans</u>	<u>French Veterans</u>
- Mr. Charles Shay	- Mr. Louis Fortin
- Mr. James Sappier	- Mr. Pierre de Fontnouvelle
- Mr. George Thompson	- Mr. Pierre Bartet
- Mrs. Thompson	- Mrs. Colette Bollens
- Mr. James Hill	- Mr. Robert Jacob
- Mrs. Hill	- Mr. Maurice Pairel
- Mr. Michael Hill	- Mr. Robert Phillips
- Mr. John Kerner	
- Mrs. Gwen Kerner	<u>French Military Mission</u>
- Mr. Henry Langrehr	- MGal Jean-Luc Delon
- Mrs. Arlene Langrehr	- Colonel Joel Rode
- Mr. Rader	- Colonel Minjoulat-Rey
- Mrs. Rader	- CDR de Felcourt
<u>French Chancery/Consuls</u>	- SGM Alain Bordedebat
- Laurent Delahousse	- SGM Martial Payen
- Etienne de Gonneville	- SMSgt Cordelier
- Michel Schaffhauser	- MSgt Bouton
- Francois Gauthier	- Mrs. Patricia Fauvel
- Philippe Ardanaz	- Mrs. Evelyne de Bernardo
- Pierre-Francois Mourier	- Mr. Manuel de sa Cunha
- Jean-Baptiste de Boissiere	

14h00   Depart French Embassy for Reagan National Airport
16h00   Take-off
Escort: Sergeant Major Alain Bordedebat

The group from Boston was very punctual and arrived at 11:00 as
scheduled. Of course, by this time, there was complete confusion, reporters
trying to do interviews, cameras running, and me trying to entertain my

illustrious guest. Although we were never able to enter the house, I did manage to take François into the teepee and explain a little bit of its history to him. Reporters continued to interview and cameras continued to roll until it was time for us to leave for the community center.

Chief Kirk Francis introduced the consul general to the Tribal Council and other guests, presented him with a gift from the Penobscot Indian Nation, and then invited all to a buffet that had been prepared.

At 13:00 hours we were driven to Bangor International Airport, where François Gauthier, James Sappier, and I boarded our flight to Washington, DC, with a stopover in Boston.

In Boston we were joined by George Thompson and his wife, of Milton, Massachusetts. He was also a WWII veteran and was accompanying us to Washington to attend the ceremony. Our flight was uneventful, and on arrival at the Washington air terminal we were greeted by military members driving limousines of the French *corps diplomatique* and taken to the Park Hyatt Hotel in Washington, DC.

Our first evening in Washington was at our leisure, and after locating Chief Kirk Francis, who had arrived before us, we decided to meet at 20:00 hours in the dining area for dinner. I talked with my son, Jonny, who was staying at another hotel, and asked him and my grandson, Ian, to join us for dinner. We spent a very enjoyable evening together, just randomly discussing past and upcoming events.

6 NOVEMBER 2007

Today was to be a very busy day for all concerned. I had been in contact with Harald and Bunny, who were staying with Bunny's father. He lives in the Washington area. We coordinated our

To Charles Shay – With admiration and respect for your service to our country! Best wishes!
Sen. Susan Collins

plans to ensure that all would be present at the residence of the French ambassador not later than 15:00 hours. President Nicolas Sarkozy was scheduled to arrive at 15:45, and when you have an appointment with the president, one does not keep him waiting.

Before I left Maine, I had been in touch with the office of Senator Susan Collins, and arrangements had been made for me to be present in her offices in Washington at 10:00 to greet her and to receive her congratulations for the award that I was to receive from President Sarkozy later that same day. I was accompanied by the entire entourage from the Penobscot Indian Reservation, who had been invited to be present in Washington for the ceremony, including my son and grandson.

Following our visit with Senator Collins, we returned to our hotel to prepare for the grand ceremony that afternoon. All seven veterans with their family members and friends were staying at the same hotel, and we were to be taken to the ambassador's residence in a fleet of limousines of the *corps diplomatique*, being driven by high-ranking enlisted men from the embassy's office of the defense attaché. Everything proceeded precisely and on schedule. I was one of the first to enter the residence, and I was

GROUP PHOTO WITH NANCY PELOSI

greeted by name by the welcoming warrant officer, Dany Herbert-Schinzel, who showed me where I would be sitting during the ceremony.

We still had approximately one hour before the arrival of His Excellency

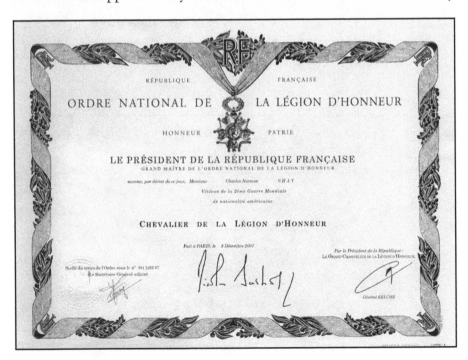

Nicolas Sarkozy, and this offered the opportunity to be introduced to and talk with many interesting people. Word was then received that the president was arriving shortly, and we were instructed to take our assigned seats. I must confess that there was some confusion and much excitement circulating through the audience, and suddenly the president made his entrance, preceded by members of his delegation. All were standing in respect. He immediately went to the podium, and the ceremony was underway. Following his opening statement, he addressed each of the seven veterans individually, citing what each had accomplished during WWII and proclaiming each a hero who had defended and freed his country and the rest of Europe from a reign of Nazi oppression.

President Sarkozy then stepped down from the podium and advanced
to the first man to be awarded the medal of the Légion d'honneur, who
in this case was no other than the Honorable Daniel Inouye, senator
from Hawaii. The president then proceeded down the line, pinning the
award on the tunic of each individual, drawing each to him, touching each

other's cheeks, left and right, made eye-to-eye contact, and gave a gripping
handshake. I was very impressed with the gratitude and the sincerity of this
man. This was an occasion which I shall never forget. I have never been
treated with such graciousness in my entire life. Following the pinning
ceremony, we all posed for a group photo, so that all would have a lasting
memory of this momentous ceremony.

His Excellency disappeared as quickly as he had appeared. I had brought
gifts to be presented to the president and to the ambassador in the name
of the Penobscot Indian Nation, but never had the opportunity to do
so personally. The presentation was conducted through a representative.
Following the ceremony, I was interviewed by reporters of the French
media. I think these interviews were only because I was a Native American.
There was a buffet with very delicate French canapés and excellent French
champagne, and at approximately 18:00 hours we were again escorted back
to the hotel. Chief Kirk Francis closed the day by inviting the Penobscot
Indian Nation entourage for dinner that evening.

FRENCH PRESIDENT NICOLAS SARKOZY DECORATES SEVEN WWII VETERANS IN WASHINGTON DC

Despite a very heavy, if not hectic, program, French President Nicolas Sarkozy took time off from his official schedule to personally honor American Veterans who took part in France's liberation during the Second World War. Later that day, as I thanked him for making this significant effort, he told me that nothing was more important than honoring those men who had come across the ocean to free France. Some, he said, never made it back. They lie in French cemeteries; they are some of the heroes of this Greatest Generation who made the ultimate sacrifice to free Europe from the Nazi oppression. Those who survived are worthy of the same respect, admiration and gratitude. I could tell that the French President was truly emotional about personally attending the ceremony, which took place at the French Ambassador's residence in Washington, and I am gratified to see that under his leadership French American relations and friendship have never been stronger. Thank you Mr. President!

President Sarkozy's speech follows:

"Mr. Senator, Ladies and Gentlemen, it is my very great pleasure to welcome you to the French Ambassador's Residence. You were 18. You were 19. You were 25. You had barely entered adulthood. Yet, that was the age at which you found yourselves engaged in the worst war in the history of humanity. Your engagement was heroic. From Hawaii, a victim of the Japanese Air Force, to the beaches of Normandy, from the siege of Lorient to the Vosges, the Ardennes and the entry into Germany, you experienced the harshest ordeals. If Europe lives in peace today, it owes it to you. Thus, as President of the French Republic and Grand Master of the National Order of the Legion of Honor, I want to express today, on behalf of the French people, our profound admiration and our immense gratitude.

Senator Daniel Inouye, you enlisted in the 442nd Regimental Combat Team, a unit composed entirely of Japanese-American soldiers. You distinguished yourself in the Vosges during the rescue of the "Lost Battalion." As Senator of Hawaii, you have played a key role in scientific cooperation between France and the United States.

French President Nicolas Sarkozy speaks during a ceremony where he awarded seven US WWII veterans the French Legion of Honor Medal, Tuesday, Nov. 6, 2007, in Washington. (AP Photo/Haraz N. Ghanbari)

Sergeant James Hill, you were in the 29th Infantry Division. You landed with the first wave on Omaha Beach on June 6, 1944. You helped liberate Saint-Lô, fought in the Battle of Vire and helped liberate Brittany. You often say that France has a special place in your heart, and you have returned there often. And the French intelligence services have done a good job, because I happen to know that those are French cattle you are raising in Tennessee!

John Kerner, you are the oldest here. Sixty-three years ago, you were a surgeon in the 35th Infantry Division. You landed with the second wave on Omaha Beach. You cared for French and German soldiers. You followed your division until it met up with the Red Army at the Elbe. Like your two friends, you are a hero.

Henry Langrehr, a parachutist in the famous 82nd Airborne, you were parachuted over Normandy during the night of June 5-6, 1944. You took part in the battle of Saint-Mère-Eglise, the first French village to be liberated. Wounded outside of Saint-Lô, you were captured and sent to work in a German coal mine. You managed to escape and return to the Allied lines. Henry Langrehr, you are a hero.

Bernie Rader, you suffered from poor eyesight, so you learned the eye chart by heart in order to enlist! A foot soldier in the 94th Infantry Division, you took part in the Normandy campaign and the liberation of Brittany. You were wounded during the siege of Lorient and taken captive. You were then released during an unprecedented prisoner exchange organized by the Red Cross. Bernie Rader, you are a hero.

Charles Shay, you were in the 1st Infantry Division. You were part of the first wave on Omaha Beach. Several of your comrades were wounded, and you pulled them out of the water yourself. You saved your comrades despite the danger. You went on to serve in the Korean War, where French and American troops fought side by side under the banner of the United Nations. You are also a Penobscot Indian, and I would like to pay tribute to your Nation. You are a direct descendant of Chief Joseph Orono, an ally of George Washington during the Revolutionary War. You are also the [descendant] of a French trapper. The ties that bind you to France thus go back to the 17th century. Basically, you have been French much longer than I have!

George Thompson, a mortar-man in the 90th Infantry Division, you arrived in Normandy on June 8, 1944. You were wounded in August in the fighting around the Falaise Pocket. You rejoined your unit very quickly for a long and dangerous march that took you from Normandy all the way to Czechoslovakia. Like your comrades, you are a hero. I want to tell all seven of you that France will never forget what you did for us. I have come to tell you that in France, there are many white crosses where lie some of your comrades who did not return to the United States. Know that their memory is cherished by all the people of France. I want to tell you one thing: The sacrifice made by you and your comrades was not in vain. And if I am here before you, it's because men like you did their duty. And I want to say to your families that they can be proud of you. We will never forget what you did for France."

French President Nicolas Sarkozy, center, stands with World War II recipients of the French Legion of Honor Medal. From left: Sen. Daniel Inouye, D-Hawaii; James Hill of Elora, TN; John Kerner of San Francisco; Henry Langrehr, of Clinton, IA; Bernard Rader, of Freeport, NY; Charles Shay of Old Town, ME; and George Thompson of Milton, MA. (AP Photo/Haraz N. Ghanbari)

TOP: FRENCH LEGION OF HONOR. ROW 2: SILVER STAR, BRONZE STAR FOR VALOR WITH TWO OAK LEAF CLUSTERS (2ND AND 3RD AWARD), POW MEDAL. ROW 3: COMBAT MEDIC BADGE WITH STAR (2ND AWARD, WWII, KOREA).

THE LEGION OF HONOR

After the French Revolution had abolished all the old royal orders (including the Order of St. Louis, founded by Louis XIV in 1693), it was soon realized that some form of official compensation was needed to honor outstanding service.

The First Consul Napoleon Bonaparte, seeing himself as the heir of the Revolution, conceived the formation of an honorary order that would reflect the principle of equality not only between military and civilian personnel but also in services rendered to the country. Napoleon's project was adopted by the law of 29 Floréal, Year X (May 19, 1802), under the name Legion of Honor.

From the outset the First Consul, then Emperor, intended membership in the Legion of Honor to be a distinction of such illustriousness that it would fire people's imagination, spur soldiers to valor and be held in high esteem in other countries. With the head of state as its Grand Master, the Legion of Honor would be conferred on individuals in all walks of life — the military, magistrates, administrators and civil servants as well as men of distinguished achievement in the arts, fine arts, teaching, agriculture, trade and industry.

On July 15, 1804, the first medals were awarded in the Church of the Invalides with all the splendor of imperial pomp. The Emperor personally bestowed the awards on members of the great bodies of state — the assemblies, judges, clergy, the Institute — and on the marshals and soldiers of the garrison in Paris. During the 1st Empire, the vast majority of appointees were soldiers, but civilians of merit did not go unrecognized. Some of the most illustrious names in France at the time appear on the lists, learned men like Monge, Chaptal, Bertholet, Jussieu and Montgolfier; artists David, Gérard and Houdon; and among foreigners, Goethe. Some are less famous, such as Hubert Goffin, a simple miner who received the insignia of the Order from Napoleon I in 1812.

The Legion of Honor was retained during the Restoration and coexisted from 1814 to 1830 with the old royal orders that were revived. At that time, it went to many civilians. Victor Hugo and Lamartine were made knights in 1825. Then starting with the reign of Louis Philippe, the Legion of Honor became the sole French national order, and the awards instituted by the kings disappeared for good. In 1962 General de Gaulle signed a new Code which, while taking into account the evolution of ideas and manners, restored the Legion of Honor to the character it had at its inception.

The Legion has three ranks: knight, officer, commander, and two dignities: grand officer, and grand cross. A second national order, the National Order of Merit, was instituted in 1963.

DESCRIPTION OF THE LÉGION D'HONNEUR

HARALD PRINS, IAN AND JOHNNY SHAY, BUNNY McBRIDE, CHARLES SHAY, KIRK
FRANCIS, JIM SAPPIER.

7 NOVEMBER 2007

Today was our last day in Washington, and the schedule was full up to
the time of departure. We were to be picked up at our hotel (with luggage)
at 08:45 to be taken to the Capitol to attend President Sarkozy's address
to the 110th Congress, which was scheduled for 11:00 hours. On our
arrival, we were escorted to an ornate waiting room where we were to be
welcomed by the Honorable Nancy Pelosi, Speaker of the House, and to
pose for a group photograph.

At the conclusion of President Sarkozy's speech, we were escorted to
the French Embassy restaurant for lunch, which was attended by U.S. and
French veterans, French chancery diplomatic team members and consuls,
and members of the French Military Mission.

At 14:00 hours, we departed the embassy for Reagan Airport to board
our flight, which was to take us home again. We were escorted by Sergeant
Major Alain Bordedebat, with whom I still have e-mail contact and who
has promised to visit our Penobscot Indian Reservation with his family. I
hope to be able to greet him in the summer of 2008. In spite of the fact
that the past six weeks have been at times exhausting, I must confess that I
will miss all of the excitement and the attention. I now return to my lonely
life with my newly found memories.

In conclusion, I now include a copy of the certificate I received from the Ambassador of France to the United States, that attests that I am now a Chevalier de la Légion d'honneur, with his sincere congratulations.

I was invited to be present at Fort Riley, Kansas, from 27 to 30 October 2008, for ceremonies where I was inducted with six other veterans as a DMOR, Distinguished Member of the Regiment. The DMOR Investiture Ceremony took place on the 27th.

I spent the following weekend visiting with Harald and Bunny, who have a beautiful house on a large plot of ground at Manhattan, Kansas, only a few miles from Fort Riley. While there, I visited the Flint Hills of Kansas and the campus of the Kansas State University, and on Monday, 3 November 2008, I returned to my home on the Penobscot Indian Reservation.

It was an impressive affair and a great privilege for me to be recognized with this coveted honor. I was able to make many new friends among the veterans and also became acquainted with friends of Harald and Bunny, who made me feel at home.

During WWII, in all branches of the military, there were eighty-five young men and women—almost all of whom were volunteers—from our small reservation of five hundred people. Three of these volunteers were killed in action: Donald Francis, David Sapiel Jr., and Byron Sockalexis. At this time, we as a people were denied the right to vote in federal, state or local elections by the state of Maine. We were, however, required to register for the draft, under penalty of the law if we did not comply. We were considered "wards of the state," which therefore placed us in the same category as criminals, paupers, and morons. We as a people finally gained the right to vote in federal elections in 1954, and state and local elections in 1967.

I recall returning to the reservation following my release from the military service at the end of the war, only to find that conditions had not changed from that time when I had entered military service in 1943. Hoping for a better life, I returned to the military and retired at the early age of forty in 1964, after having served twenty years—ten years with U.S. Army and ten years with the U.S. Air Force.

I would like to dedicate this short autobiography encompassing my military service to the three Penobscot Indians who paid the ultimate price, to all Penobscot Indian veterans, and to my people of the Penobscot Indian Nation.

II

Autobiography of Charles Norman Shay

I, Charles Norman Shay, and my brother Patrick Joseph were born in Bristol, Connecticut. I was born on 27 June 1924 and my brother Pat on 7 May 1926. I was the eighth of nine children of Leo Shay and Florence Nicolar. My mother lost her first child, Sylvia Louise Shay (born 27 July 1908, died 26 October 1908), and one son, Winter Andrew Shay (born 15 July 1909, died 10 February 1925), probably in Connecticut, as a result of appendicitis.

My parents, who had been working in Waterbury, Connecticut, were caught up in the stock market crash of 1929, and because of lack of work were forced to move back to their home on Indian Island. At the time, I was approximately four years old and do not remember much about our move back to the origin of my parents.

As I was already of the age when I would soon be required to attend school, for reasons unknown to me my mother selected me as the first one of our family to attend the Herbert Gray School in Old Town, Maine, from the first grade onward. The reason probably was that the school on the reservation was being taught by the Sisters of Mercy, and my mother was of the opinion that too much emphasis was being placed on religion and not on subjects that would prepare us for higher education. My mother wanted very much that one of her seven children would eventually attend college, but that was not to be. The war changed many lives.

Being an Indian boy in a class of approximately forty other children was difficult for me, but I eventually made many friends and soon became an accepted classmate. My younger brother Patrick attended the school on the Indian reservation and didn't follow me to the Herbert Gray School.

Because of my mother's stance on the parochial school on the reservation and other problems involving the church, it came to a confrontation. The residing priest condemned the actions of my parents from the pulpit during a Sunday morning service, and my parents with other members of the family arose and walked out of the Catholic Church, never to return.

However, my mother was baptized and raised in the beliefs of the Catholic Church, and without this spiritual guidance in her life, which she missed very much, she was lost. It was then that my mother with other members of the family and the children attended the Protestant Churches of Old Town. First the Methodist Church and then the Baptist Church, where we became accepted members.

Because this group wanted their own church on the reservation,

HERBERT GRAY SCHOOL ROOM

negotiations began with the Baptist Diocese to have a Baptist minister assigned to the reservation. Our first Baptist minister was the recently ordained Reverend Jesse Starr, accompanied by his wife, Myrtle, and their newborn daughter, who joined our community in 1940. My parents took them into our home until other arrangements could be made for them.

The building where the Protestant church is now located was at one time the old town hall and was falling into complete disrepair. The current town hall was located farther down the street, directly across from the Catholic church. Arrangements were made to take charge of the old building with the property, and work immediately began to rebuild and convert the old town hall into the first Protestant church on the reservation. Reverend Jesse Starr, who was originally from the state of Georgia, became a carpenter, and he with my father, Leo Shay, and my brother, "Billy" Shay, and other members of the community soon had the building adapted to a place of worship that also included very comfortable living quarters for the new pastor and his family. Strangely enough, the congregation grew quite rapidly. This whole process left a lasting impression on my life, because we were looked down upon for leaving the Catholic Church by other members of the community and by the children who had been and whom I still considered to be my friends. It was a difficult time for me and my brothers.

I was raised in the old homestead of the Nicolar family, and Ada Sockabeson was our neighbor. Ada, who lived alone but had a friend by the name of John Boyle, an Irishman, had no running water in her home, and I used to carry water from our house and also chop and carry wood for her. John Boyle, who was a cook for loggers in the Maine woods, stayed with Ada when he came out of the woods, and would pay me for taking care of Ada and doing small chores for her. We had to be careful, however when he gave me money that Ada didn't see how much I was getting. It seems that she always had to know what was going between the two of us.

As a young boy, I can remember when some of us boys would greet the white tourists who visited the reservation to see the Indians, how they lived, what they looked like, and to buy handmade baskets and novelties produced by them. All of the boys of my age took turns greeting the visitors, acting as a guide for them, and then performing an Indian dance, if they wanted to see us perform. This was our way of picking up a few nickels and dimes. I have no idea what the other boys did with their earnings, but I saved mine and eventually was able to purchase my own (and first) bicycle from Sears department store.

My father, Leo Shay, by the tent at Lincolnville Beach.

Also at this time many of the boys of my age had a small .22-caliber rifle. Because my parents did not have money for such things, I had to earn the money to buy my own rifle. I would go hunting for rabbits and partridge with friends of mine. We would also set snares out for rabbits. In the winter when we had a lot of snow, the rabbits always traveled the same route in the snow, and the snares, made of wire, were set on these trails with brush left and right of the trail, so that when the rabbit was traveling his accustomed route, he would become entangled in the snare. We had to remember where our snares had been laid out, so that we could find them the next day and collect a rabbit or two. I was very proud when I knew that the meal that was placed on the table the next day was there because of me.

I can also remember that I was very attached to my mother, and as a young boy I would help her with household chores by washing and scrubbing the hardwood floors in our home on Saturday afternoons, while she was making baskets and listening to afternoon concerts on the radio in an adjoining room. Sometimes I would buy my mother a present for Mother's Day or Easter with money that I had earned. It was usually a small box of chocolates. I would also wash my sweaters and iron my pants on weekends, so that I would look presentable when going to school on Mondays.

My mother and father had set up a small tent on the reservation to market the baskets that they made and other Indian novelties, but because so many people of the reservation were doing the same thing, my parents began looking for a location somewhere along the coast of Penobscot Bay, where there would be more tourists and less competition. They eventually

WITH MY BROTHER PATRICK (LEFT) AND OUR FATHER, LEO SHAY.

found the ideal spot at Lincolnville Beach, six miles before Camden, Maine. It was a plot of ground which they were able to rent for a reasonable fee, directly across from the beach and a lobster pound, on Route 1. However, because they could not finance a wooden structure to be used as a small shop, they purchased two canvas tents, which were set up end to end, one to be used as a sales room and the other for living quarters. Actually if one looks to history, this was a custom passed down for generations.

It was a difficult time for my mother and father with two small boys. We had no water or electricity, but fortunately there was a public water pump nearby, and kerosene was used for light and heat. Also we had no toilet, and we had to use a pail which was half filled with water and had to be emptied each day. We found a place where we could do this, but it was embarrassing for me anyway, because I knew that people were sometimes watching us. As business increased, my parents were able to rent a small apartment from the landlord, and we were able to live more comfortably.

The year was 1931; I was seven and my brother was five, and my parents did this every year until the beginning of WWII, setting up the tents in the spring and dismantling them in the fall. At the age of ten, I went to Rockport Golf Club, about ten miles from Lincolnville Beach, to work as

A VISITOR AT THE TENT WITH MY PARENTS, FLORENCE AND LEO SHAY.

PENOBSCOTS DRESSED FOR A PAGEANT, 1931; BACK ROW: LEO SHAY, HOWARD RANCO, ROLAND NELSON; FRONT ROW: BRUCE POOLAW, LUCY POOLAW (PRINCESS WATAHWASO), FLORENCE NICOLAR SHAY; AUTHOR IN FOREGROUND.

a caddy, hitchhiking both ways daily, and I continued to do this until we stopped going there during the war.

The year was 1939, and WWII had already started in Europe, although at the time it was not identified as such. The United States was already gearing up for a confrontation with Nazi Germany, and they were only waiting for a reason to enter the conflict. On 7 December 1941, the Imperial Japanese Navy, using aircraft carriers, made a devastating attack on Pearl Harbor, and the way was open, first by declaring war on Japan and eventually joining our allies in Europe in their struggle for survival. The National Socialist government of Germany had prepared its war machinery diligently and conducted a blitzkrieg that overran most of its neighboring countries in short order. The rest is history. However, this unprovoked attack by the Empire of Japan changed the world and the lives of millions. Perhaps unbelievable and hard to understand, even our small Indian reservation was affected by the events that were taking place.

Shortly after my parents had returned to their ancestral home, my mother's sister, Lucy Nicolar (Princess Watahwaso), who had been traveling the theater circuit throughout the country performing recitals, legends, songs and dances in costume with her husband, Bruce Poolaw, was also

Charles Shay
(Little Muskrat)

forced to return to our small Indian Reservation for lack of work. But they soon discovered that they could continue this way of life by visiting hotels and summer camps during the summer and fall to entertain the guests in the evening by with Indian songs and dances. Part of the agreement at these engagements, where they depended on donations as pay, was to be permitted to set up a table, where Indian articles such as baskets, moccasins, and novelties could be displayed and sold. I often participated as part of the entertainment team as an Indian dancer and was always introduced to the audience as Little Muskrat or sometimes as Charlie Muskrat.

CHARLES SHAY AT GRADUATION FROM OLD TOWN HIGH SCHOOL, 1942.

I can also remember that during this period (1930–1942) there was much poverty among the Indians on our small reservation. We were living in isolation with no connection to the mainland, except by boat or canoe. In the winter we were able to travel to the mainland by walking over the frozen river. This, however, was problematic in the fall and spring, when the ice was unsafe and very dangerous. As we had no food or clothing stores on the reservation, we were dependent on the businesses in Old Town. Because our young men had no employment, alcohol was also a problem. When war was declared on Japan and eventually with Germany, the young men and women of the reservation saw this as an opportunity to break away from this way of life by enlisting into the military service. From our small population of five hundred individuals, eighty-five young men and women eventually joined all branches of the military service. When the war came to an end and these volunteers returned to their ancestral home, the situation had not changed. We still lived in poverty, and employment in local businesses was practically nonexistent.

I graduated from Old Town High in June of 1942, just short of my eighteenth birthday. At that time, President Roosevelt had introduced many programs to provide work for people. The PWA (Public Works Administration) provided work for the older generation and was responsible for introducing the sewer system, a network of street lighting, and paving the few roads that we had at that time on our reservation. The CCC (Civilian Conservation Corps) was responsible for the cleaning up and preserving the forests, among other conservation projects (my brother Billy was a member of this group). The NYA (National Youth Administration) permitted young men and women leaving high school to learn a trade in aviation, machine and foundry, nursing, etc. I chose to attend the Machinist and Foundry Training Center at Dexter, Maine, and after five months I was issued a certificate as an apprentice machinist. However, because I had to register for the draft, I was not a good candidate for employment and was unable to find work.

I did not want to enter the military service voluntarily, because I supported my mother's view that doing so endorsed an unjust policy concerning reservation Indians in Maine. That policy required our young men to register for the draft, under penalty of the law if we failed to comply, even though we had no right to vote in state or federal elections. We were second-class citizens in our own country. I joined my parents in Charlestown (Boston), Massachusetts, to await my draft call to report for military service. My mother and father were both employed in the Navy's Boston construction and ship repair facility, helping to support the United States war effort (I find this ironic). It seems that the Native American, regardless of his own predicament in having to fight for his legal rights, felt dedicated to assist in the war effort as we have always done throughout the history of this country. It is a known fact that immigrants, Italians, German, Polish, and others, had more legal rights than Native Americans during this period of time.

In April of 1943, I was ordered to report for military service. I was drafted into the U.S. Army. I reported to the Fort Devens replacement depot and was sent to Blackstone, Virginia, for basic training. Six or eight weeks later I was transferred to Fort Benjamin Harrison, Indianapolis,

Indiana, and received training as a surgical technician. In September I was on my way to Europe aboard the *Queen Elizabeth*, which had been converted into a troop transport ship. She was able to transport thousands of troops at one time and was very fast, making her a difficult target for German submarines.

After spending a week or so at a replacement depot, I was eventually assigned to the 1st Infantry Division, 16th Infantry Regiment, 2nd Battalion, as a medic. Little did I know that I was now a member of one of the most prestigious infantry regiments in the history of the U.S. military service. The 1st Infantry Division had already participated in the North African and Sicilian campaigns and was now training and preparing for the invasion of the European continent. I was proud to become acquainted and be trained by these battle-hardened veterans. I was able to learn very much from them. I learned how to conduct myself in combat and how to treat my wounded comrades under intense gunfire, among other important things.

On 5 June 1944, the time for our rendezvous with the German forces arrived. We boarded our transport ships that would carry us across the English Channel, and it was on this ship that I was about to experience an unexpected surprise. Unknown to me, Melvin Neptune, a fellow Penobscot, who was attached to the 1st Inf. Div., 26th Inf. Regt., 2nd Bn., was on the same ship. Although there were hundreds of soldiers on this ship, he somehow found out that I was there. He must have known that I was with the 16th Inf. Regt. Anyway, we had a tearful and emotional reunion traveling across the English Channel on our way to Omaha Beach. Our conver-

St. Anne's Church and rectory

DOWN STREET, INDIAN ISLAND.

sation centered upon fellow Penobscots whom we had grown up with and who were now in all branches of the military service. We were wondering where they were and what they were doing. Although Melvin and I were always within a few miles of each other throughout the European campaign, we did not see each other again until the war was over and we had both returned to our small Indian Reservation. We had both survived.

On 25 March 1945, I was taken as a POW by the German army and was released a few weeks later—on 18 April 1945, to be exact. I arrived home unannounced, and when I knocked on the door, it was opened by my mother. You can imagine the joy of my parents when they saw that I had arrived home safely. Shortly after I was released, the war came to an end.

After a brief vacation with my parents, I was sent to Lake Placid, New York, for four weeks of rest and recuperation. I was then assigned to the U.S. Army Hospital at Fort Story, Virginia, as a surgical technician in the base hospital. My job in this position was to clean and sanitize the operating room, hold patients in a position for spinal injections, and keep a count of sponges that were used during the operation, to ensure that nothing had been left in the wound once it was ready for closure.

On 27 October 1945, I was discharged from the army and returned home. My parents were still living and working in the Navy Yard in Boston when I joined them. I found a job with the Boston Sears, Roebuck & Company mail order department, but somehow I was not happy with this work.

In the spring of 1946, I left my job and went back to the reservation. I soon found out that the situation on Indian Island had not changed. Even though ninety-eight percent of our young people had volunteered or were forced to join (through the draft system) the military service during WWII, they had been denied the personal satisfaction to improve their way of living on our small Indian reservation once they had returned. They were still denied the right to participate and vote in federal, state, and local elections. I know that other veterans throughout the state who had returned home from WWII were probably experiencing their own problems, but in their situation the act of discrimination was not a factor. Poverty and lack of work still existed, and it was then that I decided to reenlist in the U.S. Army, where I was recognized for my accomplishments and not because of my heritage, religious or political beliefs. It was difficult to be a Native American in the state of Maine, and I saw no opportunity of this situation ever changing in the near future.

Within a couple of weeks, I was on a troop transport ship

796TH MILITARY POLICE BATTALION, VIENNA, 1947.

again, on my way to the continent of Europe. I joined the 1st Infantry Division at Regensburg, Germany, and worked in the Housing Office.

The Housing Office at this time was responsible for finding and confiscating homes and apartments, complete with inventory, for those families that were now beginning to arrive in Europe. It was disheartening to see families dislodged from their homes because these were needed for other purposes, but the old saying goes that the spoils of war belong to the victor.

In December 1946, I was transferred to Vienna, Austria. I had never heard of the city or the country before this date, because of my ignorance. Even though there was much devastation in the city as a result of bombing raids during the war, I was captivated by its beauty, still evident, in spite of the destruction that had been inflicted on many of

CHARLES SHAY IN VIENNA, AUSTRIA.

the landmarks and residential areas. The citizens were diligent in clearing rubble and preparing for reconstruction.

Once in Vienna, I was assigned to the Vienna Area Command (VAC), to work in a supply-and-housing unit, where I was doing the same thing that I had been doing in Regensburg. I was eventually transferred to the clothing warehouse for a couple or weeks and then moved on to the unit that was responsible for supplying American families with ice (no refrigerators), bread and milk. This was an opportunity for me to become acquainted with the German language, because I worked with young local citizens, many of whom did not speak English. It was similar to an immersion course in the language, and I was soon able to communicate, perhaps primitively, in the German language. I worked at these minor jobs for a few months until it was discovered that I was a medic, and I was eventually transferred to the medical detachment of the 796th Military Police Battalion. I was a corporal at the time.

LILLI BOLLARTH SHAY

It was also during this time, shortly after my arrival in Vienna, that I met Lilli Bollarth, the woman who was eventually to become my wife. As a child, I used to go to the local movie theater in Old Town, and two of the actors who played in operettas, Nelson Eddy and Jeanette MacDonald, prominent movie stars of that period, made a very positive impression on me. I was infatuated with the music (which, if I remember correctly, was from Franz Lehár, a Viennese composer, but who was unknown to me at the time) and by the beauty of Jeanette MacDonald, an Irish strawberry blond. Lilli was working as a waitress in a restaurant, and the first time I saw her she reminded me of Jeanette MacDonald. I knew then that I had found the woman I was looking for and that someday she would be my wife. We married on 21 March 1950, a beautiful spring day in the city Vienna. We were able to purchase an apartment through the efforts of Lilli, which remained in our possession until we moved back to the Indian reservation to live permanently in 2003. However, our life of being together as man and wife was short-lived. Soon after marrying I was transferred to Salzburg, Austria. Because the end of my tour in Europe was coming to a

LILLI AND CHARLES (OPPOSITE) IN CASABLANCA, MOROCCO.

close, I received orders in July of 1950 to report to Fort Devens at Ayer, Massachusetts. I had to return to Vienna to make arrangements for Lilli to travel with me, and because time was so short, we had to take a taxi back to Salzburg. My new wife and I traveled to Bremerhaven, Germany, and we boarded a transport ship that would take us to Boston, Massachusetts, with a stopover in Casablanca, Morocco. Here we were able to go ashore and see some of the sights of the city. It was most interesting for both of us. For Lilli because she had never been outside of Austria and for me because it was my first (and only) visit on the African continent.

We were met in Boston by my mother, who had driven from Lincolnville Beach to greet us and to escort us back to Maine. Of course the reunion and the opportunity for me to introduce my wife to my parents were emotional and a very happy occasion. We spent a few days with my parents, and in August 1950 I reported to Fort Devens, with my wife in tow, and joined the 3rd Infantry Division, 7th Infantry Regiment, 2nd Battalion Medical Detachment. Upon joining I was informed that we would be on our way to Korea in a very few weeks.

We rented a room in the home of an elderly lady and were able to spend a few days together before my departure. My mother and Lilli were at Fort Devens to see me off. When the train pulled out of the station, I waved goodbye to both of them, wondering if I would ever see them again.

Lilli stayed with my parents in their house in a room that I had completely renovated for her, and she took a job at the local shoe factory. With the money that she saved, plus the dependency allowance that she received from me, she was able to return to Europe to spend Christmas of 1950 with her family in Vienna, only six months after leaving.

At the end of September 1950, I boarded a troop transport ship in San Francisco on my way to Korea, with stopovers in Honolulu and

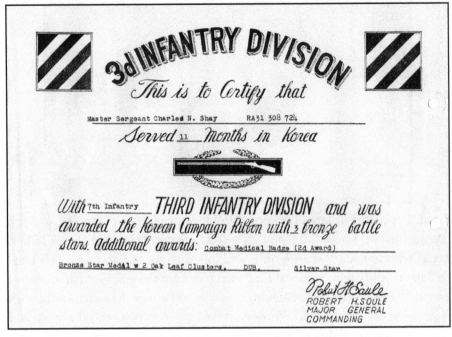

3RD INFANTRY DIVISION CERTIFICATE OF SERVICE IN KOREA

Japan. I will now relate an incident that took place in Honolulu. We had been given shore leave for the evening, and as this was strictly a sailor town, it could only mean trouble if you didn't mind your own business. Sometimes soldiers and sailors do not mix very well. Anyway, I was sitting at the bar of a night club having a beer when suddenly a fight broke out, and before I knew what was happening, I was punched in the face and also became involved in the brawl. Within minutes the navy shore police were on the scene, got the fight under control, and we were all loaded into vans and transported to the brig. That was the first and last time I ever saw Honolulu.

The next day we were on our way to Japan; we docked in the small port of Sasebo on the Island of Kyushu. We were transported up into the mountains of this island, where we would spend the next weeks training and preparing ourselves for the war in Korea.

We lived in a tent city, and occasionally we were able to go to a small military base located in the valley and order a big steak with a few beers and also visit the Japanese town of Beppu. In the middle of November, we were ordered to break camp and pack. We boarded a troop transport ship in the port city of Beppu, and we were on our way to Korea. On the 17th

TRAINING IN JAPAN

of November, 1950, we disembarked at Wonsan, North Korea, to fight a rearguard action to assist elements of the 1st Marine Division to withdraw from the Chosin Valley, where they had been isolated by the Chinese forces, who had by this time entered the Korean War. We had to control the escape route to Hamhung and the sea, where we were all evacuated by the troop ship again.

The operation was a success, but I do not know the number of casualties. I served eleven months in Korea, participating in a number of major skirmishes. I returned to the U.S. in December 1951 with the men with whom I had entered Korea. My next duty station was again Fort Devens. My wife joined me there.

A few weeks later, I was transferred to Fort Sam Houston, San Antonio, Texas. We had our own car at that time, and we planned a route that would take us from Fort Devens, Massachusetts, to Jacksonville, Florida, and then along the Gulf of Mexico, passing through Mobile, Alabama, and New Orleans, then Houston, and on into San Antonio. I reported for duty at Fort Sam Houston and was told that I would be joining the 37th Infantry Division at Camp Polk, Louisiana, and this is when I rebelled.

I'd had my fill of infantry divisions, and I made the decision to take an honorable discharge and say adieu to the U.S. Army after

A BUDDY AND ME IN JAPAN

DEPARTMENT OF MILITARY SCIENCE AND TACTICS
Office of The Professor of Military Science and Tactics
4305 ASU Texas ROTC Instructor Group
University of Texas Medical Branch
Galveston, Texas

15 April 1952

Major Wilfred T. Tumbusch, MC
Brooke Army Medical Center
Fort Sam Houston, Texas

Dear Major Tumbusch:

M/Sgt. Norman Shay, RA 31308724, has been interviewed today in reference to position as Administrative Assistant to PMS&T.

I would consider him as acceptable for this position. However, I have suggested to him that he
might well discuss the situation with you inasmuch
as his future duties at this institution will in all
probability be concerned primarily with you.

Following your conversation with him I would
appreciate a letter from you as soon as feasible in
reference to your preference on his acceptance for
this position. This will enable me to forward the
required letter to the Commanding General, Headquarters, Fourth Army, concerning his acceptability
for this position.

Sincerely,

PAUL W. HAYES
Lt Col, MC
PMS&T

LETTER FROM COL. HAYES TO MAJ. TUMBUSCH ABOUT MY INTERVIEW FOR
POSITION IN ROTC INSTRUCTOR GROUP AT THE UNIVERSITY OF TEXAS.

having served faithfully for approximately ten years. This was a difficult
decision for me, because I was leaving a secure life with no idea what the
future would hold for "us." I have to say us, because my wife was part of
my life now. However, she supported me in my decision.

I had to consult the army administrative unit that had control over me
and informed them of my decision and also asked if I would be permitted

to remain at Fort Sam Houston until my discharge, which was still a few months away. It was agreed that if I could find a job that was commensurate with my rank as master sergeant, I would not have to go to Camp Polk.

I was able to find a job as 1st sergeant in a medical training unit until the date of my discharge. While working at this job I was selected for an interview for the position of administrative assistant to the professor of military science and tactics, ROTC Instructor Group at the University of Texas Medical Branch, located in Galveston, Texas. I was interviewed by Lt. Col. Paul W. Hayes and found to be acceptable. But Col. Hayes was soon to leave this position, and he suggested that I discuss this matter with his replacement, Major Wilfred T. Tumbusch, who was a member of the Brooke Army Medical Center at Fort Sam Houston at that time, stationed at the same army base where I was working. It was a moment of uncertainty for me, first because my discharge from the U.S. Army was approaching and second I thought that Major Tumbusch might have somebody in mind that he would prefer to have as his assistant for this position. I, therefore, dropped the matter and continued on my planned course, accepting a discharge from the U.S. Army. I also knew that I was passing up the opportunity of a lifetime, because this position would almost certainly have led to a promotion to the warrant officer category. However, I had to abide by my convictions and hope that I was making the right decision. This whole affair was very unusual, considering I was a member of the U.S. Army, and normally I would not be able to go against regulations, let alone find my own job.

I was officially discharged from the U.S. Army on June 24, 1952, and we immediately undertook a long vacation by driving from San Antonio to the Grand Canyon and then west across Death Valley, up to San Diego, along the coast of the Pacific to San Francisco, and across the Golden Gate Bridge, across the Rocky Mountains to Salt Lake City, Chicago, Detroit, and into Canada through the area of the Thousand Islands, Montreal, Quebec, down to Maine. Our trip ended at Lincolnville Beach, Maine. We had a small charcoal burner and made our own meals when we found a nice spot in the wilderness, bathed in streams where we had some privacy, slept in the car, and occasionally we stayed in a motel. It was a very interesting and romantic trip for us.

Once we arrived at Lincolnville Beach, we had nothing to do, so we decided to stock up with baskets and moccasins, and we headed for the resort areas of the White Mountains of New Hampshire to try our luck at what the Indians called "peddling baskets." This involved asking

WITH MY MOTHER, FLORENCE, LILLI, AND MY FATHER, LEO.

permission of the management at upscale resorts to set up a table in the lobby of the hotels and sell baskets and moccasins to the guests. We did a very lucrative business.

We then decided to go back to Vienna, where I hoped to gain some sort of employment to support us. At this time air travel was just becoming popular, but we decided to travel by ship and booked our ocean crossing on the SS *United States* for the middle of October 1952. We still had our apartment in Vienna, which we had purchased in 1948, so we had a place to live.

The only type of work I thought I was capable of doing in a strange environment was as a private chauffeur for a wealthy family or a widow. I had two or three interviews, but no luck at gaining employment. As I had enlisted in the Air Force Reserve after my discharge from the U.S. Army, I decided to return to the United States and request recall to active duty. Lilli was not able to accompany me until I was able to get squared away with my reenlistment and find a place for us to live. I reported to Mitchell Air Force Base, Long Island, New York, and went on active duty on 9 February 1953. I was sent to the 1600th Air Transport Wing at Westover Air Force Base, Springfield, Massachusetts. Lilli then joined me in the early spring of 1953.

I had several different assignments during my active duty tour with the U.S. Air Force. After the arrival of my wife, I was sent to the 1360th USAF Hospital at Orlando, Florida, for a few months. My next duty station was with the 6th Weather Squadron on 24 November 1954 at Tinker Air Force

Base, Oklahoma, to accompany a weather reporting unit as a medic to the Marshall and Caroline Islands for Operation Castle, an atomic bomb test at the Eniwetok Proving Grounds in the Pacific Ocean.

Once again my wife and I were separated. We seemed to be having trouble staying together. Perhaps this was responsible for making our reunions and our need for each other more intense. While in the Caroline Islands, I had a chance encounter with the elders of the island where I was stationed who spoke the German language, a result of the colonization of some of the islands in the Pacific by the Germans in the nineteenth century. Upon my return, my wife was waiting for me at Tinker Air Force Base, and I was assigned to the USAF Hospital at Mitchell Air Force Base on Long Island, NY, for a few months. I was then transferred to the 2259th Air Reserve Flying Center at Byrd Field, Sandston, Virginia.

My parents visited us there in 1955 for Christmas and New Year. We visited Williamsburg and the Jamestown Settlement with them and drove up into the Blue Ridge Mountains at the time of the changing foliage. It was a beautiful trip and a great experience for my parents, for Lilli and for me. We celebrated New Year's Eve at the base hangar with music and dancing, and the next day we had invited German friends that we had become acquainted with and celebrated into the night again. This was the last time that I had such a close relationship with my parents. The following year I was transferred to Wiesbaden, Germany, where I remained for the next four years. My mother passed away shortly after Mother's Day 1960.

While at Byrd Field, I often visited the administrative offices of the U.S. Air Force Headquarters at the Pentagon and was able to gain myself an assignment to the 7100th USAF Hospital at Wiesbaden. It was always my goal to return to Europe under any circumstances. As this was a very sought-after assignment, I was fortunate to have been able to manage it, but accomplished it only through my perseverance.

Our son, Jonny, was born 5 October 1959, and this occasion made the family complete. It is one of the wonders of our world to see a helpless squirming little human being come into our world, that cries when it is hungry and dirty and is content when it is clean and has a full stomach, and to experience the progress from complete dependence, to sitting, crawling, walking, talking, and eventually to complete independence.

While we were living in Sandston, Virginia, we had purchased a little Dachshund, six weeks old, and he went to Europe with us when I was transferred to Wiesbaden. While in Sandston, I trained him to keep an eye on and guard our laundry when it was hung out for drying. He would

SON JONNY AND DOG TINO

lie under the laundry all day, driving off any birds that tried to land on the laundry lines. He never forgot this training, and after we had moved to Germany he would lie under my car that was parked in front of the apartment, and if someone walked by to close to the car he would shoot out barking at that person to scare them off. When we brought Jonny home

from the hospital, little Tino (the dog's name) took up his post under the bed of the baby and never allowed anyone into the room except Lilli and me. I recall one evening that we wanted to attend a movie, so we asked the mother of our neighbor to babysit for us while we were gone. The baby had been bathed and well fed before we left, and we knew that he would sleep through the night. However, after we left, Mrs. Harper thought that she would check on the baby and probably hold him a bit. She only got to the door of the room, and little Tino shot out barking and would not allow her to enter. When we returned, she related her experience to us and was very upset.

Jonny now has his own family and is well situated in life. He completed his schooling in Vienna and wanted to join the military service, air force, so I had to take him to Ramstein Air Base in Germany to arrange his enlistment. We returned to Vienna, and within a week or two he received notice to report to Ramstein Air Base again for his swearing-in ceremony. He was nervous and perhaps reluctant to leave us, but knew that he had to make his own way in life.

He spent approximately eight years on active duty and then was caught up in the 1989–1990 reduction of armed forces. He attended the University of New Mexico and graduated with a bachelor's degree and then returned to Vienna and enrolled in Webster University, which had set up an extension in the city, where he earned a master's degree in international

LILLI AND JONNY, COLORADO SPRINGS, 1961.

JONNY SHAY, WIFE URSULA, SON IAN CHARLES SHAY.

relations and management *(Magister der Politikwissenschaft und Management)* on 21 May 1988.

After his release from the military service in 1992, he was able to gain employment as an electronic engineer with the Federal Aviation Administration in Bangor, Maine, where he worked for approximately five years. He then transferred to T. F. Green Airport near Warwick, Rhode Island, where he is still working at the time of this report.

He continued his education through an online program, Bernelli University International Graduate School, and was awarded the degree of doctor of philosophy in social services with a concentration in international studies. He continues his military service with the Rhode Island National Guard and is enrolled in a warrant officer program; after completing the necessary training he will soon be sworn in as a warrant officer of the National Guard of Rhode Island. His wife, Ursula, is presently enrolled in the University of Rhode Island, studying radiology and hopes someday to work in a hospital where she can put her knowledge to good use. My grandson, Ian, enters his senior year in high school in the fall of 2008. I have no idea what his intentions are once he graduates from high school, but I hope he will continue his education. In today's world, an education is of utmost importance. I will never know how he will make his way through life, but I want to wish him much success and much happiness in life. (*Lieber Ian, bleibe Brav und Fleissig und viel Glück im Leben. Ich liebe Dich, dein Opa*). Both my son and grandson are black belt recipients in karate, at the chapter of Warwick, Rhode Island. Ian is in the first phase of obtaining a pilot's license.

After four years at this assignment, Wiesbaden, Germany, I was transferred to the 615th USAF Dispensary at Colorado Springs, Colorado. We were able to visit and spend a few days with my father before I had to report for duty. I had shipped my car back from Europe, and we picked it up at the port in New York and then drove from Maine to Colorado over the now famous Route 66. It was a beautiful trip, and when one approaches the Rocky Mountains from the east, the view is awesome. We rented a house from a family that was very active and owned many businesses in the area. In addition to a couple of houses, they were also owners of a two motels, a dine-and-dance club for young people, and also had the beer concession of one of the larger beer companies in the Colorado Springs area. We both worked for our landlord.

Lilli was in charge of the employees working in the motels, and I was responsible for the motel grounds, cutting grass, and doing handiwork on weekends, and acting as doorman in the evenings at the dance hall. We were doing very well financially, and that is when we began to form plans for my retirement, with the thought in mind of building a house, once I retired to Vienna. Retirement was moving up very fast, and I would soon retire from the military after twenty years of service, at the age of forty.

Colorado is a beautiful state with many points of interest, and we were able to visit some but not all of them. Colorado Springs lies almost one mile above sea level. We lived in Manitou Springs, only a short drive from Pike's Peak, and the Garden of the Gods was nearby. We visited the Royal Gorge and made several trips to the surrounding areas, to picnic and enjoy the beauty of the mountainous terrain.

My next and final assignment before retirement was back to Sembach, Germany, with the 38th USAF Hospital, 38th Missile Wing. We again rented a house in a German Village, and Lilli's mother joined us. After

almost a year at this assignment, I finally decided to retire. It was again a big decision, because although we had our apartment in Vienna, I would need an income to supplement my retirement pay in order to live the way we were accustomed to living.

I finally retired from the military service on the 31st of July, 1964, and drove immediately to Vienna, which was about a ten-hour drive. After our arrival, we were busy making arrangements to purchase a plot of ground outside of the city limits and soon found what

BUILDING OUR HOUSE AT MARIA GUGGING, OUTSIDE OF VIENNA.

we were looking for, about twelve miles from the city, near the town of Klosterneuburg.

Already in September of 1964, I was preparing the grounds so that construction of the house could begin. In the surrounding areas of the city of Vienna, it is not uncommon for families to build their own homes

LIVING ROOM OF THE FINISHED HOME AT MARIA GUGGING

after meeting certain stipulations and regulations of the local building code. Before the first snow arrived, I had, with the help of an uncle of Lilli, cemented out the foundation, and the walls of the first floor had been erected. All work was done with cement, cement blocks, and cinder blocks. Wood was only used for decorative purposes, doors and door frames, windows and window frames, and of course closure of the house with a roof. It was a difficult project, because I was building on a hillside, and proper measures had to be taken to ensure the stability of the house and the grounds. As soon as spring arrived and the ground had thawed out, construction was again started. By August of 1965, the walls of the second floor were completed and the roof was installed by the construction engineer that I worked with.

There was still very much work ahead to make this place livable. However, in September of 1965 I was contacted by the personnel department of International Atomic Energy Agency and informed that I had been confirmed for employment, and I accepted. House construction had to take a back seat, and from this time on I was only able to work on weekends, holidays, and during vacation.

The house was finally completed in the year of 1972 and completely furnished, and we began spending the holidays such as Christmas, New Year's, Easter, and weekends, and much of the summer months there. Subsequently, I was talking with a friend who I worked with. She and her husband were Americans, and she told me that she was going through divorce proceedings and was looking for a place to live. I discussed this with Lilli, and we came to the conclusion that we would move out of the apartment and rent it to her. From that time on we lived permanently in the house, and when our friend found someone else and eventually moved out of the apartment, we continued to rent (not on a permanent basis), when we found someone who was dependable.

To get back to my employment with the IAEA, I was able to gain the position only through the intervention of the United States representative to the International Atomic Energy Agency in Vienna. After I had submitted my application for employment, I was invited for an interview with the director of the personnel department, Ms. Inge Hausner-Streitenfels, a German national. At the first meeting we had a very good connection to each other, and she advised me to seek the assistance of the U.S. Representative to the IAEA. Fortunately he was also a former veteran and supported me in my application. I did not need any more. Within a few days I received notification that I should visit with the secretary of the deputy director of personnel, and I was informed that I was being assigned to the Division of Publications. It was here that scientific books and documents were published and distributed to the embassies, to members of the delegations, and also mailed directly to the appropriate office of the member states in their home countries. In the early 1970s all systems in the IAEA were computerized. I continued to work with the Publications Division, Documents and Distribution Unit. Eventually our mailing lists also went into the computer system, and once we learned how to operate the new system, it simplified our work.

In September of each, year a General Conference with delegates of all member states was held, sometimes in Vienna, and on occasion the IAEA was invited to hold their conference in the major city of one of the member states. I was always in attendance for the General Conference in Vienna and was also able to attend two such occasions outside of Vienna, one in Salzburg, Austria, and the Annual General Conference in 1979, which was held in New Delhi, India. When this conference came to an end, many of my colleagues had made plans to vacation and to visit interesting sites of India and neighboring countries, such as Kashmir. I, however, saw this as an opportunity, even before I left Vienna, to purchase objects of value that

I could enjoy long after the project came to an end. I purchased Kashmiri carpets, lamps, etc., many of which I still have in my home on the Indian reservation. My son has most of the carpets, many of which have never been laid out on the floor, because they are too beautiful and hang on the walls, at one time in my home and now in his.

I retired from this organization in December of 1984. In the spring of 1985, I received a call from the director of personnel of the IAEA asking me if I would be interested going back to work for the high commissioner for refugees, Vienna Office. They were looking to replace their security officer, who was going into retirement, and he had suggested me for the job. I went for an interview, and one of the requirements was to be fluent in German and English. I had no problem with this requirement. I was accepted and worked an additional two-and-one-half years, finally retiring in 1988.

In the year of 1987, I became acquainted with a man who had a franchise with Cary International Limousine Service, New York, through my son, who was in Vienna at the time and was looking for work. We went to the offices of the limousine service, where he had an interview and was accepted for a job. Then the proprietor turned to me and asked if I would be interested in working for him. He was in need of drivers who could speak English and German. I told him that I already was working for the

THE AUTHOR AT IAEA CONFERENCE, NEW DELHI, INDIA, 1979.

THE TAJ MAHAL

United Nations, but I could work for him on weekends and holidays, if he would be satisfied with that arrangement. We both agreed, and I worked with this limousine service until 1997, when I finally retired from all work at the age of seventy-two years.

Lilli and I had been returning to the U.S., Indian Island, from Europe at least once a year for vacations and to visit with family members. In the year of 1988 the property that I now occupy was empty after a long legal process, and my brother Bill asked me if I would like to take it over. If I would accept his offer, he would sign off all rights, and it was up to me to make arrangements with the other members of the family. I accepted. However, I had to pay some of the people concerned, and that involved a few thousand dollars. The property and buildings were in poor condition, and from 1988 onward Lilli and I spent our summers here on the reservation, repairing buildings and property. At the end of September, we would return to Vienna for the winter, where I continued to work for the limousine service, driving throughout the country of Austria and neighboring countries, depending on the wishes of the client. Such engagements included Germany, Hungary, Czechoslovakia, and Poland. I was able to meet some interesting people.

Among my clients were Steven Spielberg, wife Amy Irving, and son,

AUTHOR WITH STEVEN SPIELBERG AND WIFE AMY IRVING AND SON MAX.
BELOW: WITH A CLIENT'S ROLLS ROYCE.

little Max; Woody Allen, wife Mia Farrow and family; former Ambassador to Austria Roy Huffington from Texas, who often visited privately (he always requested that I be his chauffeur) after he had retired and always met with Kurt Waldheim, former secretary-general of the United Nations

and former president of Austria, who was also retired at this time. They often visited a district of Vienna known as Grinzing, once a village on the outskirts, now included with the city's expansion. This is a quaint part of Vienna and sits below the hilly vineyards of many private wine producers, who established small wine houses in the village, where one can sit and drink the latest vintage and enjoy a buffet of excellent food, either hot or cold, and just discuss the events of the day with company.

It was in this atmosphere that Kurt Waldheim and Roy Huffington talked with each other about the predicament of Waldheim, who had been placed on the watch list of the United States because of the connection he had to the Nazi regime when he had been a lieutenant in one of the occupied countries. For his actions there he was denied entry into the United States. This I find very strange because when his name came up to be confirmed as secretary general of the UN, with headquarters in New York City, he was supported by the United States Government. I was aware of this because I had often heard the conversations that were going on in the back seat of the vehicle that I was driving. This is the first time that I have ever spoken about these conversations, because it would have been a breach of trust if I were still working as chauffeur for the Cary Limousine Service.

Another one of my guests was the Emir of Qatar, who often visited the city of Vienna with his family during the summer months to escape the heat of his own country. (He always had two limousines for his large family.) When we delivered him and his family to the airport for their return home, he presented each chauffeur with an envelope which contained a very generous tip.

In 1998 my wife had a bad fall and broke her hip. Thereafter she had difficulty climbing stairs, and we decided to move back to the apartment in Vienna. The house stayed empty for a period of time, except for weekends and holidays, and we finally made the decision to sell the house.

The final transaction took place in the spring of 2000, and in the spring of 2001 we began making plans to move back to the Indian reservation, to the home that I now own here. We had the bulk of our furniture and other furnishings that we could not part with shipped back in 2001 and made our final move of closing down and vacating the apartment that had been in our possession for over fifty years.

In the spring of 2003 we returned to Indian Island to live permanently, but unfortunately by this time Lilli was seriously ill. She died on the 5th of September, 2003, three months after we returned. My dreams of finally

Author's home on Indian Island

being retired and spending our remaining days together were not to be. After her death, she was laid out in the teepee for twenty-four hours, and the next day a ceremony was held in the church. She was Catholic. I had her cremated according to her wish, and I have established a monument in her memory in one corner of my garden.

It was a very sad time for me. She had been my companion, lover, and supporter for fifty-seven years. Throughout this time, she had supported me in all endeavors, financially, physically, and morally. We were a good team. She has now joined our ancestors, her own and mine, and I know that she is happy and looking down upon me and waiting for me to join her.

Since her passing, I have immersed myself in our culture, promoting and keeping alive the memory of our ancestors. I have been active in the publishing of books concerning family members. They are *Princess Watahwaso: Bright Star of the Penobscot*, by Bunny McBride; and *Florence Nicolar Shay: Penobscot Basketmaker and Tribal Advocate*, by Kate Kennedy. I have also been active in republishing *The Life and Traditions of the Red Man*, by my grandfather Joseph Nicolar, father of Lucy and Florence Nicolar. I supported Annette Kolodny, professor and author, University of Arizona, who had the vision to have Joseph Nicolar's work republished by Duke University Press. Also included in this edition is a brief history of the

GARDEN MONUMENT TO LILLI SHAY, ON INDIAN ISLAND.

Penobscot Indian Nation, who we are, where we live and come from, and what our contribution to the history of this state and this country has been.

After a complete renovation of the teepee, I had the walls painted with murals by a talented young artist of the Penobscots; I engaged Calvin Francis to do the painting after I had seen some of his work. This was the largest project he had ever attempted. Calvin, my wife and I sat together to discuss what we envisioned, each with his or her own opinion. We came to the conclusion that he would start by placing family members in various positions on the walls from photographs that I provided. It was a long and tedious job, much longer than any of us thought it would be. He continued with the scenery of the Penobscot River valley and the placing of animals that are common to this habitat.

Sometimes we would look through magazines to find animals that appealed to us, and Calvin would place them on the walls. It all worked out so perfectly, and when Calvin and I or other guests observe the finished job, we still admire the work that he has accomplished and still find it to be awesome. I had a visitor the other day, and he referred to Calvin as the "Michelangelo of the Penobscots," which impressed me so very much, and I will continue to use this remark when I have visitors. Calvin is also a wood carver and musician. He still works for me when the teepee has to be refurbished and touched up on the outside walls at least every second year, because of the harsh weather we have here.

In my home I have tried to introduce a combination of European and Penobscot Indian culture, and it has come together very nicely. This, of course, is my own opinion. I have no idea what other people think when they visit me.

Having lived in Vienna for over forty years of my life with my wife, it is not possible for me to forget these years and I must confess that I think back often of our life together in the beautiful Austrian city. Since Lilli's death, I have visited Vienna three times, but have not been back since my last visit in the spring of 2005. It is not the same for me anymore. I hope to make one more visit in the near future, as long as I am still able to make the long trip. In June of 2009, I will visit Normandy, France, and Omaha Beach for the celebration of the 65th anniversary of that fateful day. I hope to combine this trip with a visit to the beautiful city of Vienna. This, in all probability, will be my last visit to Vienna. After all, I will be almost eighty-five years old.

I have received a formal invitation from the Association Béarn-Acadie-

PRINCESS WATAHWASO'S TEEPEE AFTER THE RESTORATION

Nouvelle France to visit the French city of Pau and surrounding area, following my visit to Normandy in 2009. This region was the home of Jean-Vincent d'Abbadie de Castin, who was a young French officer at Fort Pentagoet (now Castine, Maine). Jean-Vincent became acquainted with the great Penobscot Chief Madockawando in the seventeenth century. This relationship led to the marriage of Jean-Vincent to Mathilde, one of the daughters of Madockawando. Mathilde died a few years later, and Jean-Vincent then married the chief's daughter Marie. He may have had as many as ten children with Mathilde and Marie, some of whom went to France to live, while others remained in the so-called New World. This French-Indian relationship is the reason for my invitation, and it is hoped that this relationship can be rekindled.

The plan is that I will be accompanied by Chief Warrant Officer Danielle Herbert-Schinzel, a member of the diplomatic corps of the French Embassy, Peter Schinzel, a member of the delegation of the military attaché at the Austrian Embassy (both in Washington, DC), and James Eric Francis, tribal historian of the Penobscot Indian Nation. Peter and his wife, Danielle, will be moving back to Vienna in December 2008, where Peter will take on new duties, and we will meet in Paris, when I travel to Europe in 2009 to attend the ceremonies remembering June 6, 1944, Omaha Beach. We will then continue on to Pau, where we will be joined by James and Tanya Francis.

The death of my wife has left a void in my life that has not been easy for me to forget or cope with, but as I have stated above, being active in keeping the memory of my ancestors and my wife alive has somehow helped me to bridge this difficult time. I look forward to the day when I will join my wife and my ancestors in the spiritual world.

III

Return to Omaha Beach and
French Indian Ancestry

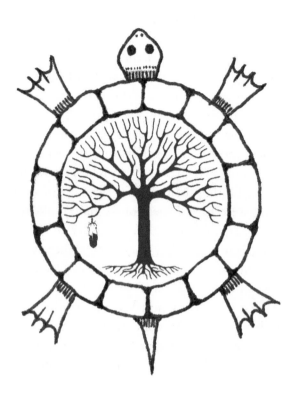

In November 2007, when I was inducted as *chevalier* (knight) of the French Légion d'honneur, I met Danielle Herbert-Schinzel, one of the members of the military attaché's section of the French Embassy. I met her after the ceremony was over and talked with her and other members of the military attaché's delegation; she expressed a desire to visit the Penobscot Indian reservation because she had visited other reservations in the U.S. I thought we were just talking and didn't pay much attention to it at the time; I didn't think they would really come to the Penobscot reservation. In April 2008, I received an e-mail from Danielle telling me that she and her husband had made plans to visit the reservation in May, for four days. I was very surprised that they were coming and made arrangements for them to stay at the Black Bear Inn.

When the time came for their arrival, they picked up a rental car at the Bangor airport, and we drove to their hotel, so they could freshen up after the flight from Washington, DC. I had prepared a light lunch for them, so after we dropped off their bags, they came to my home where we had coffee, cakes and pastries. We discussed what to do during their visit here. I had made arrangements for James Francis, the tribal historian of the Penobscot Nation, to give them a PowerPoint presentation about the history of the Penobscots from the 1600s (and the arrival of the baron de Saint-Castin), to inform them what the French-Indian connection has been over the past four centuries, and this they enjoyed very much. The chief, Tribal Council, and family members gave the Schinzels a reception at the Community Building, which was even attended by reporters from the Bangor Daily News. During their stay, we visited various nearby sites of interest. While they were here, I mentioned that I'd like to revisit Omaha Beach on June 6, 2009, for the 65th anniversary of the Allied invasion. Their immediate reply was that they would travel there with me.

However, in the meantime, in December 2008, Danielle retired and her husband, who was with the Austrian Embassy and also a military attaché, was recalled to take a new position in Vienna, Austria. They moved back in December 2008 to Vienna. We continued to correspond by e-mail and managed to finalize our plans to visit Omaha Beach. I left my home on the 1st of June 2009, flew to Paris. They left via automobile and drove to Paris, and they were waiting for me when I arrived. We left immediately for Normandy, where we had booked reservations at Le Haras de Crépon, the very old château from around the 16th century. I had stayed at the same château when I visited Omaha Beach in September 2007 with Professor Harald Prins and his wife, Bunny McBride. I already knew the proprietress, and she gave me the same room I had had the first time I stayed there. From there we were able to drive around the area and become acquainted, so we would know where to go on the 6th of June.

Many of the leaders of the Western World had been invited to the ceremonies: these included U.S. President Barack Obama, Prime Minister Gordon Brown of England, Prince Charles of England, and the French president, Nicolas Sarkozy, among others. Because of the prominence of these visitors, security was very tight and very strict. Being a veteran of WWII and Omaha Beach, I was invited with other veterans from this period to sit on the podium behind the speakers. Sarkozy was the first one to speak, opening the ceremonies, followed by Barack Obama and the other delegates who were present. Obama gave a very moving talk. The ceremony closed in the afternoon at about 16:00 hours. Strangely enough, about a half an hour after the ceremonies ended, it began to rain. We had been very lucky.

On the 7th of June we left Normandy, because I had received an invitation to visit Pau in France and the small village of Saint-Castin, the home of my ancestor, the baron Jean-Vincent d'Abbadie de Saint-Castin. This visit was organized by Madeleine Duboé, an American from Lewiston, Maine, who had traveled to France approximately twenty-five to thirty years ago to teach in a school. She was married there and stayed, although she continues to visit her family in Lewiston.

On a visit to Lewiston in August 2008, she met with a colleague, Todd Nelson, principal of the elementary school in Castine; they had been instrumental in establishing an exchange program between the students of Saint-Castin, France, and the students of Castine, Maine. Our connection was made on the occasion of her 2008 visit. I had become acquainted with Todd through an interview that he did for the Christian Science Monitor about my participation in Operation Overlord, the invasion of Europe that took place on Omaha Beach. He also knew that I was a descendant of Jean-Vincent. Todd e-mailed both James Francis and myself, to see if we would like to come down to Castine and meet Madeleine.

During my conversations with Madeleine, we discussed the French-Indian relationship of the baron de Saint-Castin and my connection to him. Jean-Vincent d'Abbadie de Saint-Castin married the daughter of Chief Madockawando of the Penobscots. Madockawando, who lived from 1625 to 1698, was probably the grandson or great-nephew of the famous Penobscot Chief Bessabez, who welcomed Samuel de Champlain in 1604. Madockawando's daughter, Mathilde, and the baron de Saint-Castin were married in 1678. Mathilde died shortly after their marriage, and soon thereafter he married her sister Marie. He had about ten children with the two Penobscot sisters.

Jean-Vincent's daughter Brigitte had a son named Joseph Orono, after whom the town of Orono, Maine, is named. Orono was famed as "the blue-eyed chief." Joseph Orono and his wife (name unknown) had a daughter, Mali Susep Orono. Mali became the wife of Captain John Half-Arm Nicola. Their son, Tomer Nicola, married Mary Malt Neptune, the daughter of Lieutenant John Neptune. Mary and Tomer had a son, Joseph Nicolar, my grandfather.

Joseph Nicolar and his wife, Elizabeth Josephs, had three daughters, Emma, Lucy, and Florence. Florence married Leo Shay and had nine children, of which I was the next-to-last born in 1924. This makes me, Charles Shay, seven generations removed from the French baron; interestingly enough, I am the only one in my immediate family to have blue eyes—like Joseph Orono, and perhaps like the baron himself.

Credit is due here to Distinguished Professor of Anthropology Harald Prins of Kansas State University, who did extensive research on family connections between the baron de Saint-Castin and the Penobscots.

It was because of this connection that I was invited by the Association Béarn-Acadie-Nouvelle France to participate in the Tour of the Penobscot Nation Ambassadors to Béarn, France, June 7 to 11, 2009. This event was created because Madeleine Duboé had informed the association I would be in France for the Omaha Beach anniversary.

On June 7 James Francis and his wife, Tanya, came directly from the United States to Paris, where they boarded a train for Pau, via Bordeaux, to join me for this event. They were met at the station by their hosts, Jean and Nicole Renault. I was accompanied by Dany and Peter Schinzel and their hosts, Bruno and Marie-Noëlle Tisserand. My hosts were Philippe and Madeleine Duboé. The visit to Saint-Castin was organized by Arthur Finzi. Pierre Casabonne organized the visit to the General Council and the receptions in Arette and Bayonne. Jean Renault organized the visit to the château de Pau, the ceremony in Escout, and the conference in Oloron-Sainte-Marie. The photos were all taken by photographers from the Association Béarn-Acadie-Nouvelle France.

What follows here is an account of our visit to the region in June 2009, composed originally in French by Jean Renault of the Association Béarn-Acadie-Nouvelle France and translated into English by Madeleine Duboé.

Béarn Acadie Nouvelle France

Tour of the Penobscot Nation Ambassadors to Béarn, 2009

by Jean Renault

The American Penobscots arrived Sunday, June 7, 2009, in the evening. Charles Shay was accompanied by Danielle Herbert (Dany) and Peter Schinzel. Madeleine and Philippe Duboé and Marie-Noëlle and Bruno Tisserand greeted them at the Pau-Uzein Airport. James and Tanya Francis arrived shortly after by train at the Pau station, greeted by Nicole and Jean Renault.

MONDAY, 8 JUNE

10:30 AM

Isabelle Pebay, assistant curator, honored us with a guided tour of the château de Pau. A detailed museum tour which lasted two hours allowed us to visit rooms which are not usually open to the public, especially one room where all the paintings were dedicated to King Henri IV.

CHARLES SHAY, TANYA AND JAMES FRANCIS IN FRONT OF A STATUE OF HENRI IV.

CHARLES SHAY AND DANIELLE SCHINZEL AT THE CHÂTEAU DE PAU. "AMONGST ALL OF THE KINGS WHO CROWNED FRANCE'S DESTINY, HENRI IV IS WITHOUT A DOUBT THE ONE WHO WAS AND STILL IS THE FRENCH PEOPLE'S FAVORITE, 'THE ONLY KING PEOPLE REMEMBER.' THE FIRST FORTIFICATION WAS MADE OF WOOD ON A ROCK CLIFF BETWEEN THE PAU RIVER AND ONE OF ITS TRIBUTARIES, THE HEDAS. FROM THIS MODEST BUILDING, THE VICEROYS OF BÉARN TOOK ADVANTAGE OF THE NATURAL SETTING TO BUILD A VERY SIMPLE FORTIFIED CASTLE, AS OF THE ELEVENTH CENTURY" (DOC. CHÂTEAU DE PAU).

PENOBSCOT TRIBAL HISTORIAN JAMES ERIC FRANCIS RECEIVES THE CONSEIL GÉNÉRAL MEDAL FROM STÉPHANE COILLARD.

12:30 PM

We were invited to the Navarre Parliament (parlement de Navarre), home of the Conseil général des Pyrénées-Atlantiques (state government), by Pierre Casabonne, mayor of Arette and House representative (conseiller général), by Stéphane Coillard, House representative (conseiller général) of Morlaas, along with Arthur Finzi, mayor of Saint-Castin and president of our association. All of the members of the board of administrators of Béarn-Acadie-Nouvelle France were present. After a tour of the consul room, we had lunch in one of the parliament's reception rooms.

At the end of the meal, Pierre Casabonne and Stéphane Coillard gave Charles Shay and James Francis the Conseil général medal in memory of their visit.

LEFT TO RIGHT: STÉPHANE COILLARD, PIERRE CASABONNE, CHARLES SHAY, AND DANIELLE SCHINZEL.

ON THE MENU

Wild mushroom salad with duck foie gras sautéed in port wine
Monkfish rolled in bacon with a julienne of vegetables
Cheese from the valley of Ossau (south of Pau)
Cold cherry soup with Madiran wine and Bourbon vanilla ice cream

2:30 PM

Press conference with the two regional daily newspapers, *Sud-Ouest* and *La République des Pyrénées*. With the help of Danielle Schinzel as translator, Charles Shay was interviewed about his experience on D-Day 1944.

4:00 PM

Saint-Castin elementary school visit.

CHARLES SHAY, ARRIVING UNDER AN UMBRELLA HELD BY DANIEL BASSERAS, AT THE SCHOOL FOR A MEETING WITH THE CM1 AND CM2 STUDENTS (4TH & 5TH GRADES) RECENTLY BACK FROM THEIR TRIP TO CASTINE, MAINE.

Between the school visit and the memorial ceremony, Charles, James and Tanya spent a few moments of R&R at the café and restaurant, Le Castine, in Saint-Castin, where Memene and Jean-Pierre greeted us all.

After the press conference on the terrace of the Conseil Général: Arthur Finzi, Pierre Casabonne, Charles Shay, James Francis, Stéphane Coillard, and Jean Renault.

Jean-Pierre welcomes Charles Shay at Le Castine

In Sandrine Nusbaum's class, the students had many, many questions to ask Charles Shay and James Francis, who explains (above) what wigwams are, drawing on the board, while Madeleine Duboé translates.

6:30 PM

In the presence of the Harmonie Paloise orchestra and the soldiers of the 5th Regiment HRC, Charles Shay and Arthur Finzi placed flowers on the War Memorial in Saint-Castin. Many war veterans of Saint-Castin and the surrounding towns had come to pay their respects.

SPEECH BY ARTHUR FINZI, MAYOR OF SAINT-CASTIN, PRESIDENT OF BANF

Charles Norman Shay, on behalf of the citizens of Saint-Castin, on behalf of all those present tonight, I wish you a warm welcome.

Charles Norman Shay, we are honored by your visit on two counts.

First of all, you are, above all, the descendant of Jean-Vincent d'Abbadie, baron de Saint-Castin and of his Penobscot wife. Allow me to look at the history of Béarn beyond the blue through your presence. It is with great pride that we welcome you as the official representative of the Penobscot Nation. You are also one of the American Army veterans who were the first troops to land at Omaha Beach in Normandy. This last Saturday June 6th, during the official commemorations, we could appreciate the emotion linked to these

memories. I thank you, Charles Norman Shay, for having responded to our invitation. This morning you visited the city of Pau and its castle. Tomorrow you will go into Béarn to the roots of your family and finally end your journey in the Basque Country. All of these places you'll be visiting belong to you in heart. We are pleased to have you take them back with you. They represent our mutual heritage, a heritage which you helped us to preserve by accepting to come over to liberate the land belonging to France.

Thank you Charles Norman Shay.

The end of the day was spent at the town foyer at a *vin d'honneur*—a glass of Jurançon wine—offered by the Town Hall. Each guest returned to their host family's home for a light dinner and a well-deserved night's rest.

TUESDAY, 9 JUNE

10:30 AM

Unveiling ceremony at the Town Hall of Escout, presumed birthplace of Jean-Vincent d'Abbadie.

CHARLES SHAY UNVEILING THE PLAQUE, WHICH READS: *JEAN-VINCENT*
D'ABBADIE, BARON DE SAINT-CASTIN (1652-1707). ORIGINAIRE
D'ESCOUT, IL ASSURA LA PRÉSENCE FRANÇAISE EN ACADIE, À LA
FIN DU 17ÈME SIÈCLE, AVEC L'APPUI DE SES ALLIÉS ABÉNAQUIS.
[JEAN-VINCENT D'ABBADIE, BARON DE SAINT-CASTIN (1652-1707).
ORIGINALLY FROM ESCOUT, HE ENSURED FRANCE'S PRESENCE IN
ACADIA AT THE END OF THE 17TH CENTURY, WITH THE SUPPORT OF
WABANAKI ALLIES.]

BEFORE THE CEREMONIES
IN ESCOUT, JAMES AND
TANYA WENT TO TASTE
A LITTLE JURANÇON AT
A VINTNER'S, MONSIEUR
GUIROUILH. A PERFECT
WAY TO START THE MORN-
ING, ESPECIALLY FOR
JAMES WHO WAS GOING
TO GIVE A CONFERENCE
THAT SAME AFTERNOON

In the presence of Gérard Urrustoy, Mayor of Escout, Charles Shay unveiled a plaque in memory of Jean-Vincent d'Abbadie, baron de Saint-Castin. Two costumed soldiers from the seventh-century Carignan-Salières Regiment were also present. One of them was Bruno Tisserand, treasurer of our association! Arnaud de Castelbajac, a Béarnese "cousin" of Charles Shay, was among the guests.

SPEECH GIVEN BY GÉRARD URRUSTOY
MAYOR OF ESCOUT, VICE-PRESIDENT OF BANF

You visit today from the United States, a country filled with natural splendors, a country which awakens one with open eyes and open heart before its spectacular landscapes, where the great breadth of land gives a feeling of freedom.

Monsieur Shay, you tramped the French soil sixty-five years ago on June 6, 1944, with the American Army; you liberated our land. You were able to fight with great courage and bravery, so that all of humanity could find freedom. You are an honored veteran.

You are accompanied by Mr. James Francis, an eminent historian, a specialist in Native Indian history.

Today, you have crossed the Atlantic, to discover the unusual history of a young boy of Béarn, born in the middle of the

CHARLES SHAY, JAMES FRANCIS, AND VINTNER GUIROUILH.

seventeenth century, Jean-Vincent d'Abbadie, son of the lord of Escout and baron de Saint-Castin, your illustrious ancestor.

As an orphan, the young Jean-Vincent signed up for the army in 1665, bound for Nouvelle France, now known as Canada, at only the age of thirteen. He landed at Pentagoët in Acadia. There followed many years of training, and combat against the English in the French Kingdom, a vast area, home to the Wabanakis. At eighteen years of age, the young officer was given the responsibility of Fort Pentagoët by the governor of Acadia, De Grandfontaine. Little by little, Jean-Vincent gained the trust of the great chief of the Penobscots, Madockawando, whose daughter he married. Having become baron de Saint-Castin following his brother's death, he played a major role in preserving Acadia from the grip of the British Empire.

In 1696 he managed to take over the powerful Fort at Pemaquid, one of his most famous victories, which made him a permanent figure in history.

The baron de Saint-Castin died in 1707 at PAU, after a very unusual life. Today in the United Sates, in the state of Maine, a town carries the name of Castine; it was the location of Pentagoët three

PIERRE CASABONNE GREETED US ACCOMPANIED BY THE MUSKETEERS OF THE BARÉTOUS. FOLLOWING THE TRADITIONAL PHOTO ON THE STEPS OF THE CHÂTEAU D'ARETTE AND A DRINK IN THE GARDENS, WE ENDED THE MORNING AT A RESTAURANT IN THE TOWN OF ARETTE, OVER A LOVELY MEAL.

hundred years ago. In 1987 a Quebecois descendant came to Escout, Gérard Saint-Pierre, and then Marjolaine Saint-Pierre, who wrote a book dedicated to his ancestor with the help of our local historian, Bernard Cheronnet, who built up a very interesting bibliography on this subject.

In January 2003, the Association Béarn-Acadie-Nouvelle France was founded with the towns of Arette, Escou, Escout, Lahontan, Saint-Castin, and in 2005 Susmiou joined also. The objective is to perpetuate the memory of the children of Béarn, who dared to cross the Atlantic to confront the New World—to continue to shed light on the heritage linked to its pioneers and to maintain relationships and cooperation with the people, the organizations and the institutions of the regions concerned.

Today we have a website which can be consulted, thanks to the

GIFTS WERE PRESENTED IN THE GARDEN AT THE CHÂTEAU D'ARETTE.

work of Jean Renault and of a few people who haven't counted the number of hours within the association.

The first big event was held in June 2003 with the visit of Gilles O'Bomsawin, great chief of the Abenaki Nation, and his partner Beatrice Joyal.

Today, you are present to perpetuate the memory of our illustrious compatriot, three centuries and a half following the birth of the baron de Saint-Castin. As the deceased Bernard Cheronnet said, "History isn't a dead subject. Through history, people should feel that they are part of a long line, and because of this they should feel responsible for the future. *[L'histoire, ce n'est pas une chose morte. Par l'histoire, les gens devraient ressentir qu'ils font partie d'une grande lignée et, de ce fait, ce sentir responsable de l'avenir.]*

In a few moments, we will unveil the plaque dedicated to your illustrious ancestor, Jean-Vincent d'Abbadie, baron de Saint-Castin.

After the vin d'honneur (a toast with Jurançon wine) offered by the Town of Escout in a very friendly atmosphere, along with the citizens of Escout and their Mayor, we headed for Arette.

12:30 PM

A quick tour of the château d'Arette. Here stands the birthplace of the Béarn-Bonasse family, maiden name of the mother of Jean-Vincent d'Abbadie. This castle is now a private home. The owner very kindly allowed us to visit the grounds and the dining room in which there are many very old paintings and family portraits, along with beautiful ancient tableware.

OH NO, HERE THEY ARE AGAIN!

4:30 PM

The next visit was Oloron-Sainte-Marie, capital of Haut-Béarn (southern Béarn). Chantal Larrouy greeted us to tour the Oloron cathedral, a UNESCO World Heritage site. The stonework over the main entrance, particularly showing the local traditions and historical ways of life, were explained at great length before we visited the inside of the cathedral.

5:30 PM

We arrived at the Municipal Council room at the Oloron Sainte-Marie City Hall, where Bernard Uthurry, Mayor of Oloron, was awaiting our visit. It was James Francis's turn to "go to work." He gave an hour-long conference on the history and traditions of the Penobscot Nation, very well illustrated with a PowerPoint presentation and translated by Madeleine Duboé.

During the vin d'honneur (once again an excellent Jurançon!), Jean-Pierre Domecq, conseiller général and adjoint au maire (state representative and assistant to the mayor of Oloron-Sainte-Marie) joined us. We also had the pleasure of meeting Mrs. Reyau, another Béarnese cousin of Charles Shay.

JAMES FRANCIS GIVING HIS CONFERENCE. THE AUDIENCE WAS VERY INTERESTED IN THE PRESENTATION AND WERE PLEASED TO DISCOVER AN ASPECT OF THE LIFE AND HISTORY OF THE UNITED STATES OF AMERICA WHICH IS UNKNOWN TO THE LOCAL PUBLIC OF THIS AREA OF FRANCE.

TANYA AND JAMES FRANCIS WITH THE SOLDIERS FROM THE SEVENTH-CENTURY CARIGNAN-SALIÈRES REGIMENT

AT THE END OF THE CONFERENCE, BERNARD UTHURRY, MAYOR OF OLORON-
SAINTE-MARIE, GAVE CHARLES SHAY THE MEDAL OF HONOR OF THE CITY OF
OLORON.

8:30 PM

Wow, the day is finally ending! Everyone gathers, members of Béarn-
Acadie-Nouvelle France and friends, for a Béarn buffet of different
pork sausages and fresh Pyrenean cheeses with nice bread and pastries,
accompanied by the regional wines at Chez Cottet, a restaurant just outside
of Oloron-Sainte-Marie.

WEDNESDAY, 10 JUNE

Before going to the Conseil général in Bayonne, we visited Navarrenx
with James and Tanya. A tour of the ramparts was a MUST!

In Bayonne, Pierre Casabonne and Monique Larran-Lange, conseillère
générale (state representative), greeted us for a press conference (another
one!).

After a quick snack at the Conseil général bar, we went off for a tour
of Bayonne Cathedral. This tour is essential, and Monique Larran-Lange
became our very knowledgeable guide.

Tanya on the ramparts in Navarrenx, a fortified city. From its founding it was a border town. In 1188 a stone bridge was built, and a market was established. The big arch on the bridge over the Gave d'Oloron (river) dates back to the thirteenth century, but lost its defense tower since then.

We quickly crossed the village cobblestone streets through the market held that day.

Cathédrale Sainte-Marie de Bayonne

Left to right: Basque Country Museum Director Rafael Zulaïka, Pierre Casabonne, Monique Larran-Lange, and Charles Shay

Charles Shay and Peter Schinzel in Saint-Jean-de-Luz

TANYA FRANCIS AND BASQUE COUNTRY MUSEUM TABLEAU

12:30 PM

Now for a traditional Basque meal with of course a magnificent T-bone steak grilled over a wood fire and accompanied by French fries and Pyrenean cheese, with the Basque cherry jam, all of which went down very easily with the local wine and apple cider—a very happy and joyous atmosphere in a typical Basque auberge.

Following lunch we toured the Basque Country Museum, guided by its director, Rafael Zulaïka. Recently renovated, the museum is quite interesting and worth a visit. All of the local traditions and lifestyle of times past are portrayed, along with many works of Basque art.

The afternoon ends with a stop in Saint-Jean-de-Luz, a small, beautiful and quaint seaside town, with its narrow, stone-paved streets and white façades trimmed in red and green, and the heat of the day brought us inevitably to a café terrace on the town square, where we all indulged in a cool, refreshing drink!

AT THE CAFÉ ON THE TOWN SQUARE OF SAINT-JEAN-DE-LUZ

THURSDAY, 11 JUNE

It's unfortunately the end of the journey, too short a journey. We still had so many things to see and do. A last look at the château de Pau.

But it's only an *au revoir*—see you again soon.

When the association was founded in January 2003, we had set down some very ambitious objectives. Today we can say we've accomplished quite a few. The exchange program between the schools of Castine and Saint-Castin are rolling and will develop even more. The relationship between our association and other associations in the Maritime Provinces of North America are there to speak for themselves. As of 2003, we had contacted the Abenaki Nation of Quebec. This year we reinstated our relationship with the Penobscot Nation, more than three centuries after Jean-Vincent d'Abbadie. The ties had been broken over the years. Thanks to Charles's, James's, and Tanya's visit, we now have an extraordinary opportunity. *We must now try to find our common history, respectful of each one's particular character, to learn once again to know and understand one another, and I am convinced that we are all willing to do so.*

Jean Renault

Association Béarn-Acadie-Nouvelle France

JAMES AND TANYA FRANCIS WITH NICOLE RENAULT IN FRONT OF THE
CHÂTEAU DE PAU

IN THE NEWS

TRANSLATED BY MADELEINE DUBOÉ

The Béarnese Indian

A descendant of the baron de Saint-Castin, this American took part in
D-Day in 1944

by Tarik Khaldi, *Sud Ouest*, Saint-Castin, Wednesday, 10 June 2009

Sixty-five years ago, he was on board one of those U.S. landing craft,
in first line, ready to land on the Normandy beaches. Today he can
be found in the Pyrénées-Atlantiques, where he has been visiting since
Monday.

Charles Norman Shay, a Native American Veteran—one of the few—is walking the path of his ancestors. In fact, Béarnese blood flows through his veins. And not just any blood. Seven generations separate him from his seventeenth century ancestor, Jean-Vincent d'Abbadie, baron de Saint-Castin.

Baron and Indian chief

The baron de Saint-Castin is thought to have been born in Escout in 1652. He played a key role in New France in the war against the British Empire, and then against the Iroquois, after which time he returned to France.

A few years later, in 1670, the Béarnese baron returned to the land of the Native Americans—to Acadia, which corresponds today to the American state of Maine. He settled amongst the Penobscots and married Pidianske, daughter of the Indian chief Madockawando.

After the latter's death, the Béarnese baron became chief of the tribe. Before returning to France in 1700, he left the mark of his time in Acadia; the village of Castine where the baron had lived—and where Charles Shay lived—was named after him, in memory of the baron de Saint-Castin.

D-Day

Three centuries later, the baron de Saint-Castin has a number of descendants, some having stayed in America in the tribe; others went back to France or left to live in Australia.

Among those who remained in the United States: Charles Shay. On June 6, 1944, at the age of nineteen, he was sent to the front line in France, as a medic. Once he hit Omaha Beach, he spent three-quarters of the day on the beaches treating wounded soldiers. A full day under fire from the enemy. That he survived, "it's thanks to the prayers of my mother," he said.

About sixty years later, this trip back to France is emotional for him. Adorned with an Indian collar, Charles Shay considers his visit to Béarn "as a privilege."

Commemoration

Invited on Monday afternoon by Pierre Casabonne, conseiller général [state representative], mayor of Escout, and member of the Association Béarn-Acadie-Nouvelle France, Charles Shay came to talk about his origins, about his story, and that of his ancestor. By his side at the Parliament of Navarre, where this event took place, there was James Francis, a historian who specializes in the history of the Penobscots.

For Charles Shay, this tour is an opportunity to "represent the Penobscots," to celebrate the commemoration of D-Day, and to connect with his roots.

It's the first time the descendant of the baron has walked on the land of this region. Scheduled in the tour are Saint-Castin and its surroundings, Pau, and the Basque Coast. Monday at 6:30 p.m., the American Indian will go to Saint-Castin to participate in a patriotic ceremony. During his 2007 visit to the United States, Nicolas Sarkozy decorated this Native American with the highest honor, the Légion d'honneur, for the bravery his ancestor would never deny.

HISTOIRE • Réception au Parlement de Navarre

Sur les traces de ses ancêtres

Sept générations
ont passé ~~PAU & GRAND PAU~~
du baro,
revient sur la terre
de ses ancêtres.

Charles Shay a été reçu lundi au
Parlement de Navarre par le
conseiller général Pierre Casabonne, et les représentants de
l'association Béarn-Acadie-Nouvelle France. Il représente la tribu
indienne des Penobscots qui vit
dans le Maine.
  Il est accompagné par James
Francis, historien de la tribu et
professeur à l'Université du même
État. C'est la première fois qu'un
descendant du Baron de Saint-

*Charles Shay entouré par Pierre Casabonne et Stéphane Coillard,
sur le balcon du Parlement de Navarre. (Photo Marc Zirnheld)*

In the footsteps of his ancestors

Reception at the Parliament of Navarre

L'Eclaire, Wednesday, 10 June 2009

*Seven generations have passed. The descendant of the baron de Saint-Castin
came to the land of his ancestors.*

Charles Shay was invited to the Parliament of Navarre by the conseiller
général [state representative] Pierre Casabonne and the representatives
of the Association Béarn-Acadie-Nouvelle France. He represents the
Indian tribe of the Penobscots, who live in Maine.

He is accompanied by James Francis, tribal historian and professor at
the University of Maine. It's the first time a descendant of the baron de
Saint-Castin has returned in the footsteps of his ancestor.

D-Day on the Normandy beaches

In 1944 Charles Shay landed on the Normandy beaches with the American
Army. During his trip to the United States in 2007, Nicolas Sarkozy honored
him with the highest rank of honor, the Légion d'honneur. After having
participated last weekend at Colleville-sur-Mer in the commemoration of
the 65th anniversary of D-Day, he has come to Béarn for a few days.

During this visit, he will tour the places which shaped the first thirteen years of the baron's life until he left for Acadia. Following this interview in Pau, Charles Shay met with the children of the elementary school in Saint-Castin, before going to the Town Hall. Yesterday he followed a path leading him to Escout, Arette, and finally Oloron. An exceptional visit in an emotional atmosphere, it brought a whole page of the history of Béarn up to date.

An American Indian in Béarn

Inauguration of the commemorative plaque of the baron de Saint-Castin

by M.G., *La République des Pyrénées*, Wednesday, 10 June 2009, Escout

Yesterday, an American Indian descendant of the baron de Saint-Castin inaugurated a commemorative plaque in Escout.

He had travelled in the opposite direction of his ancestor. In the [seventeenth] century, the baron de Saint-Castin, born in Escout, became the chief of a North American Indian tribe.

At the age of eighty-five, Charles Norman Shay, who lives on a North American Indian reservation, came to Escout for the first time in his life to discover the land of the baron. The illustrious *Béarnais* had left to colonize America and ended up marrying the daughter of the Indian chief of a Wabanaki tribe.

Charles Shay is the seventh-generation descendant. "It was my destiny to come here," explained this member of the Indian community. The project started about two years ago and came true following "encounters, mere chance, and coincidences," he explained.

His life was marked by the Second World War. He was amongst the American soldiers who participated in D-Day in Normandy on June 6, 1944. Along with his division and while many of his comrades died that day, he set foot on Omaha Beach. He pushed on to Belgium with the American Army until he was made prisoner of war.

"For a long time, I never spoke to my children of this episode of my life, nor of my Indian origins," Charles Shay told us. But in 2007, on the occasion of his first presidential visit to the United States, Nicolas Sarkozy made him a member of the Légion d'honneur at a ceremony thanking veterans of WWII. A decoration that he wore proudly yesterday on his suit lapel. A few months later, he met members of the Association Béarn-Acadie-Nouvelle France.

With Barack Obama at Omaha Beach

The commemoration in Normandy of the sixty-fifth anniversary of D-Day in the presence of the American President Barack Obama last weekend was the trigger. Norman Shay found himself in the first row, just behind the statesmen. "It was very moving. I paid tribute to my deceased comrades that day," he said. He then took advantage of his trip to France to take a detour through Béarn and tour another location related to his story and his family. "The spirits guide us," he said yesterday during the inauguration of a commemorative plaque of the baron de Saint-Castin at the Escout community hall. He went on to visit Arette, and at the end of the afternoon in Oloron-Sainte-Marie, he participated in a conference about his ancestor.

In the footsteps of his past

Meeting with Charles Shay, the descendant of the baron

La République des Pyrénées, Friday, 12 June 2009, Saint-Castin

The village was host to Charles Shay, Penobscot Indian and glorious American combatant.

In the life of a village, there are unique moments that will remain in the minds of its people for a long time.

Monday, June 8, with great emotion, Mayor Arthur Finzi, president of Béarn-Acadie, his municipal council, and the citizens welcomed Charles Shay during his tour in the footsteps of his ancestor. He is the descendant of a famous French trapper, none other than Jean-Vincent d'Abbadie, baron de Saint-Castin, who had married the daughter of the great chief of the Penobscot tribe in 1678.

Reception at the City Hall

Arriving in mid afternoon, he visited the school and greeted the children and staff, as well as the teacher, Mrs. Nusbaum, and her students, who last May had gone to Castine (Maine, United States).

CHARLES SHAY SURROUNDED BY MAYOR ARTHUR FINZI AND THE VETERAN REPRESENTATIVE MR. LACOSTE PHOTO BY YASMINE DUMINY, LOCAL CORRESPONDENT FOR PYRÉNÉES PRESSE AND MEMBER OF BÉARN-ACADIE-NOUVELLE FRANCE.

Then he assisted in a commemoration at the war memorial, in the presence of the military and local authorities, along with veterans' representatives, with musical accompaniment by Harmonie Paloise. Mr. Shay fought during WWII. He was decorated with the Bronze Star, Silver Star and the Légion d'honneur, which he received in Washington, DC from the hand of President Nicolas Sarkozy.

He was part of the American delegation at the sixty-fifth anniversary commemoration of D-Day on the Normandy beaches.

The visit ended with a reception at City Hall, where everyone was able to talk to Charles Shay and his interpreter. Saint-Castinians discovered a man of great charisma.

At eighty-five years of age, of smooth and serene countenance and clear blue eyes, he answered with kindness and candor the many questions asked. Around his neck he was wearing a Penobscot collar with protective virtues, inherited from his mother.

After having lived a long time in Austria, Charles Shay now lives in the United States, in the state of Maine, where he resides at the heart of an Indian reservation.

Other events are scheduled, and Charles Shay, whose life merges with our contemporary history, perfectly incarnates and symbolizes the link between our two continents.

Sur la terre de ses ancêtres

Devant la porte du château d'Arette, Charles Norman Shay et Pierre Casabonne entourés des Mousquetaires et de deux représentants du Régiment de Carignan-Salière auquel appartint le Baron de Saint-Castin. (Photo Bernard Cabanius)

Charles Norman Shay fait partie des 45 000 indiens d'Amérique qui ont servi pendant la Seconde Guerre mondiale. On compte parmi eux 98 Penobscots, membres de la communauté **La République** dienne du même nom.

Charles Norman Shay comme 51 de ses frères, la « Silver Star » pour sa bravoure dans l'action. Il décida retrouver en Béarn le souvenir du Baron de Saint-Castin dont il est un descendant de la septième génération. (lire notre édition du mercredi 10 juin) Cette parenté, certes lointaine, peut s'expliquer par l'adoption, en 1670, de l'aventurier

béarnais par la communauté des Penobscot, au sein de laquelle il vécut de riches heures, aussi bien sur le plan sentimental que grâce à la pratique des fourrures. fait marout où il n Béarn Acadie-Nouvelle France puis s'est rendu à Arette.

Dans la mère **OLORON** l'édifice Béarn-Bon. Casabonne, maire d'Arette et conseiller général, accompagné d'une délégation de la Confrérie des

Mousquetaires de Béarn et Gascogne en tenue de cérémonie.

Pierre Casabonne rappela combien le Béarn était fier de l'épopée du Baron de Saint-Castin aux confins du continent nord-américain. « Une nouvelle page de notre histoire commune est en train de s'écrire », a conclu l'élu avant qu'avec **HAUT-BÉARN** ne la enobse ypique de sa tradition artisanale. Ces deux cadeaux seront bien sûr exposés à la Maison du Barétous dont l'inauguration est prévue le mois prochain.

22   Vendredi 12 juin 2009

In the land of his ancestors

After the commemoration of 6 June 1944

La République des Pyrénées, Friday, 12 June 2009, Arette

Charles Norman Shay was one of the forty-five thousand Native Americans who served during WWII. There were ninety-eight Penobscots, members of the Acadian community of the same name.

Charles Norman Shay was decorated with the Silver Star, along with fifty-one of his brothers, for bravery in action. He decided to find in Béarn the memory of the baron de Saint-Castin, of whom he is a seventh-generation descendant (see our Wednesday, June 10 issue). Though distant, this kinship is explained by the adoption in 1670 of the Béarnese adventurer by the Penobscot community in which he lived during some very rich times, in terms of the heart as well as the fur trade.

Charles Norman Shay made a lengthy stop in Escout on Tuesday, where he was received by the Association Béarn-Acadie-Nouvelle France, after which he arrived in Arette.

In the courtyard of the château, where the baron's mother had lived when it belonged to the Béarn-Bonasse family, Pierre Casabonne, mayor of Arette and conseiller général, was waiting with a delegation from the Brotherhood of Musketeers of Béarn and Gascony in ceremonial costume.

Pierre Casabonne recalled how proud Béarn was of the epic of the baron de Saint-Castin on the confines of the North American continent. "A new page of our mutual history is in the process of being written," concluded the representative, and with the dignity of a true gentleman, the Native American veteran presented him with the flag of the Penobscot Nation and a basket emblematic of traditional craftsmanship. These two gifts will certainly be on display at the Maison du Barétous [museum], which will be inaugurated next month.

Websites to visit:

http://saint-castin.jimdo.com
http://www.paysdemorlaas-tourisme.fr
http://www.musee-chateau-pau.fr
http://www.pau.fr
http://www.valleedebaretous.com
http://www.oloron-ste-marie.fr
http://www.saintjeandeluz-paysbasque.com
http://www.bayonne-tourisme.com/visites-guidees/index.html
http://bayonne.plus.free.fr/bayonne-cathedrale-rue-d-espagne.htm
http://www.musee-basque.com
http://www.bayonne.fr

HONORING OUR ANCESTORS

At the invitation of the
Association Béarn-Acadie-Nouvelle France
Salle Barthou, Oloron-Sainte-Marie, Béarn
9 June 2009

A presentation by Charles Norman Shay
Penobscot Indian Nation
Indian Island, Maine, USA

Mesdames, Messieurs!

I am honored to have been invited to Béarn, here in the foothills and mountain valleys of the French Pyrénées. The love you have for your homeland and its amazingly rich cultural heritage is inspiring.

I stand here as a Penobscot Indian elder with a bloodline that reaches back to ancestors who were among the first to welcome French mariners reaching the seacoast of Northeast America more than four hundred years ago. Living there, we are the first people in the Western hemisphere to see the sun rising out of the sea. This is why our homeland is known as Wabanaki—Land of the Dawn.

In 1604, we welcomed Champlain, who became famous as an explorer. Our ancestors did not know the purpose of his expedition, but agreed to trade furs and moose hides for iron knives, axes, copper kettles, and other useful European products.

Not long after Champlain's visit, my people made an alliance with the French, who provided our warriors with firearms to defend ourselves against enemies. For many years, we had waged wars against the Iroquois, who raided our villages and captured our women and children.

More dangerous to our survival than the Iroquois were the English colonists, because they wanted our beautiful homeland. We fought many wars to defend it, but were too small in number to stop the ever-growing number of well-armed white settlers.

Stories of those bloody wars are described in a book written by my grandfather Joseph Nicolar—stories passed down through generations and told to him by the tribal elders of his day. His book, titled *Life and Traditions of the Red Man*, was published in 1893.

One of the great chiefs who led our Penobscot warriors in their struggles for freedom was Madockawando. A successful hunter and brave warrior, this grand chief was known as a skilled diplomat who negotiated treaties with friends and enemies. I mention Madockawando because he is one of my illustrious ancestors. His life began nearly three centuries before my own. I'd like to tell you a bit about him and how his life story links your people to mine.

As I just mentioned, the Penobscots were threatened by two enemies, the Iroquois and English. It so happened that French families settling in Canada faced the same threats. Chief Madockawando had a son and a number of daughters. And that brings me to another remarkable figure, who still appeals to our imagination, both here in Béarn and across the ocean, especially in Maine. I am speaking here, of course, about Jean-Vincent d'Abbadie. The younger son of the baron de Saint-Castin, he was born near here in 1652 and died in Pau in 1707. However, Vincent spent most of his life overseas among my people. And he became Chief Madockawando's son-in-law.

As a descendent of Vincent and his Penobscot wife, I have become intrigued by this French baron's adventurous life and increasingly interested in learning more about him. Recently I've discovered a few interesting contrasts and parallels between his life and mine.

Born in great privilege, Vincent lost his mother when still a small baby. Because his older brother was in the position to inherit their father's estate and his title of baron, Vincent had to carve out his own path in life and chose a military career. If he was fortunate, he would survive and become successful and wealthy in his own right. At age thirteen, he joined the Carignan-Salières Regiment, an elite French infantry unit. Having sailed across the Atlantic to Canada, the young cadet carried the banner of his proud regiment and participated in a victorious campaign against fierce Iroquois warriors in 1666.

I myself had a less privileged beginning. I was born into a small Indian community that had lost most of its land and traditional rights. But my parents were proud and unbowed. They were among the Penobscots who led our people's struggle for survival and sovereign rights. After the Second World War broke out, their four sons, me included, all served in the military, as did most other young Penobscots.

Recruited by the U.S. Army in 1943 at age eighteen, I joined the 16th Regiment of the famous 1st Infantry Division, also known as the Big Red One. Trained as a combat medic, I entered the war in the early morning of June 6th, 1944. I was among the very first assault troops landing on Omaha Beach, Normandy. On that day in hell, I felt my mother's prayers sustaining me. She was a very spiritual woman, and that thought helped me find the strength and courage to help and rescue comrades being shot and wounded all around me. My regiment suffered enormous casualties, and many brave young men died on that day.

Coming back to Vincent, four years after his regiment gained victory over the Iroquois, he arrived on the Maine coast as part of the new French garrison at Fort Pentagoet, near Chief Madockawando's tribal headquarters. Vincent, now eighteen, became friendly with the Indians encamped nearby. Four years later, in the Spring of 1674, Dutch privateers suddenly arrived in their swift frigates, took the French garrison by surprise, and destroyed the fort. The officers, Vincent included, were captured for ransom. After a short time in captivity, he was let go to travel through the vast forest to Canada, to secure the ransom money the Dutch demanded to release his commander.

Having completed his mission, Vincent stayed only briefly among the French in Canada. Instead of going back to Béarn, he decided to return to the Maine coast, where he became a fur trader. Establishing himself near the ruined fort he knew so well, he courted the beautiful daughter of Chief Madockawando, whose name was Pidianiske.* After her baptism by a French missionary, she received a new name, Mathilde, and then married

---

*For Pidianiske's short biography, see Bunny McBride, *Women of the Dawn* (Lincoln: University of Nebraska Press, 1999).

Vincent. By then, his older brother had died in France, which meant that he had right to the family title as baron de Saint-Castin.

In my own case, after the Normandy invasion and the Battle of the Bulge, I also was captured by the enemy. After a few weeks in a German prisoner-of-war camp across the Rhine, I was liberated and briefly returned to my family and the Penobscot Indian reservation in Maine. After the war, I rejoined the American army occupying Germany, was then transferred to Vienna, where I met a beautiful Austrian woman, Lilli, who later became my wife. Although we traveled much, our home was in Vienna.

Vincent and Mathilde had many children, girls and boys. In order to claim his ancestral estate in Béarn, Vincent sailed across the ocean back to France in 1701. Mired in a family dispute over family property, he died in Pau six years later. At the time, there was another big war raging on the Maine coast. With his father gone, Vincent's oldest son, a French-Penobscot Métis named Bernard-Anselme (we do not know his Indian name) had distinguished himself as a brave warrior. With Vincent's death, Anselme inherited the baronial title and its privileges. Already distinguished as a young war chief, Anselme was appointed as a French military officer. After the war, he and his wife, daughter of a well-to-do French settler, moved across the ocean to Béarn with their daughters. Anselme held a seat in the Parliament of Navarre.

Anselme died in Pau in 1720. But Vincent's other French-Penobscot Métis children remained in North America. One of his daughters had a grandson named Joseph Orono, who was chosen as a life-chief by the Penobscot tribe and became famous during the American Revolutionary War. That great chief was the great-grandfather of Joseph Nicolar, my own grandfather, who published the book on our tribe's history.

Like Vincent, I returned to my ancestral home in the later years of my life—in my case traveling across the ocean in the opposite direction. My Austrian wife, Lilli, joined me, but to my great sorrow died soon after the move. Suddenly, I was living alone.

Then, two years ago, my life took an amazing turn. That came as a result of my decision to come back to Normandy and honor my comrades who lost their lives on bloody Omaha. The day I returned home to Indian Island from that pilgrimage, I received a call from the French consul general in Boston. He gave me news that both astounded and humbled me—news that the French president himself would induct me as a *chevalier* in the Légion d'honneur.

By way of conclusion, I would like to pay tribute to my mother, Florence.

She sustained me through her prayers in times of great danger and is my blood-link to Vincent, the brave and adventurous baron whose romantic spirit brought us all together on this wonderful day.

It has been a true privilege to be your guest, and your gracious hospitality has warmed my heart.

Salut!

Charles Norman Shay
Chevalier de la Légion d'honneur
DMOR* 16th Infantry Regiment, 1st Infantry Division

Here follow extracts from a handwritten letter by Dany Schinzel, in which she gives her account of my meeting with Michel Rougier—another descendant of the baron de Saint-Castin—who was eager to know his Maine cousin.

THURSDAY, 11 JUNE 2009

We leave Pau by plane at 10:55 a.m., waving goodbye to Madeleine [Duboé], Bruno Tisserand and his wife, Marie Noëlle. Uneventful flight (1 h, 25 min) to Paris. In Charles de Gaulle [Airport], after collecting our luggage, we take the speed Métro (RER) to Gare du Nord, where we board a taxi to the hotel. Hôtel des Arts Bastille is a small hotel with small but clean rooms. Good welcome at the reception, then a nice lunch in a Basque bistro on the other side of the street. We are still in the southwest ambiance. After freshening up in our rooms, we go by Métro to our meeting with Michel Rougier. James and Tanya should join us later, since they are coming back from Pau by train.

Great welcome by Michel Rougier, so eager to show what documents he possesses that he doesn't want even to let Charles drink a

---

*Distinguished Member of the Regiment

tea before doing so. Among all his collection, he first found a picture of the sister-in-law of Charles, then one of the whole family, including Charles's mother as a child.

A few moments later, Louis, Michel's son, arrives and starts putting questions about the great connection between the two branches of the family. Emmanuel, Michel's nephew, joins the meeting, and the two younger men seem more than interested and the talking goes on and on.

James and Tanya finally reach our crowd, and we have a light dinner (smoked salmon, salad, and ice cream) together.

The Rougiers have a great knowledge of the family tree and follow the appearance of new descendants, by blood or adoption, with great interest. They are very proud of their origins and want to keep in contact with the "cousins" of Maine. Later on, after the departure of James and Tanya who are going to see the Eiffel Tower, Emmanuel is kind enough to propose to drive us back to our hotel. Doing so, we have a wonderful tour of Paris, where we see, successively:

- Les Invalides (front and back)
- The Seine River (crossing by the bridge Alexandre III)
- The Grand Palais and Petit Palais, two famous museums
- Place de la Concorde, where a very special dinner is going on with 7,000 guests all dressed in white
- View of the Champs-Elysées and the Arc de Triomphe
- The Jardin des Tuileries
- The Louvre
- La Conciergerie, where the Queen Marie Antoinette was held prisoner before being beheaded
- The Gare de Lyon (nice train station)

Back to our hotel, we say goodbye to Emmanuel, who then proposes to take us on Saturday to visit the château de Versailles.

ON SATURDAY MORNING WE HAD a rendezvous arranged with Emmanuel, the nephew of Michel Rougier, to meet at the Arc de Triomphe. Danielle, Peter, and myself traveled via Métro, and Emmanuel met us there with his car. He drove us to his home, where his wife, children, and some of his neighbors were assembled, because they wanted to meet their "uncle," as they called me, from the Penobscot Nation. We had a very pleasant visit; Emmanuel's wife prepared lunch for us, and we had some very interesting conversations. After visiting for approximately two hours, we said goodbye to my newfound relatives, and Emmanuel drove us to the château de Versailles. He escorted us around the large, complex grounds and explained the meaning of the objects we were viewing. We spent about an hour and a half visiting the grounds of the château, and following our visit we went to a restaurant for a beer and a small lunch. This completed our visit to the château de Versailles, and Emmanuel drove us back to the hotel, where we said our goodbyes, not knowing whether we would ever see each other again. I would like to remain in contact with my distant cousins; if I should ever visit Paris again, this will be one of my homes away from home.

The next day, Danielle and Peter Schinzel accompanied me to the airport, where we also said our goodbyes. I left Paris on an eight-hour flight to Philadelphia; Peter and Dany left Paris and drove back to Vienna. This was a very interesting experience for me, one that I will never forget.

IV

Association "Deep Respect"

Association "Deep Respect"

Carole Duval and Tenno Dogger are pleased to present their association, which was founded in September 2010. Association "Deep Respect" is intended to preserve and transmit the memory of the veterans of World War II who contributed to the success of Operation Overlord.

The association provides assistance to veterans and their families in realizing their wishes; we welcome all veterans and their families. School children in the region are invited to participate in events and may adopt and sponsor projects, including:

- Installation of plaques in memory of those who have been forgotten
- Restoration and maintenance of monuments and graves abandoned and/or damaged
- Laying of flowers
- Transmission of the individual history of veterans and their families
- Veterans Week in Normandy

Please visit our website at www.deeprespect.org.

VETERANS WEEK

4-11 JUNE 2011

With Association "Deep Respect"

Association "Deep Respect"* organized a special week in Normandy for three American and four British veterans. The Americans, Steve Kellman and Charles Shay, both landed on Omaha Beach on D-Day with the 1st Infantry Division, and the British veterans, Bob Rome, Cyril Banks, Dick Morrison-Story—all three of HMS *Ready*, 18th Minesweeping Flotilla—and Eric Rackham of the Royal Army Service Corps, were for a whole week the special guests of Deep Respect.

They stayed together in the lovely villa Le Presbytère at Grandcamp-Maisy. It was very sad that the seventh member of this group, David Nelson, also from the 1st U.S. Infantry Division and who landed on the 6th of June, 1944, on Omaha Beach, had to cancel his journey a day before the departure date from the States. The emotions about returning to Normandy for the first time since 1944 were too intense, at least for this nice ninety-three-year-old man.

Carole Duval and Tenno Dogger drove to Paris and Cherbourg, to pick up the Americans at the airport and the British from the English Channel ferry. Cyril came ten days earlier, and Eric came from Australia with his wife, Gloria, on the 21st of May. The meeting was at the villa in Grandcamp-Maisy, during the evening on Saturday. Lucien Duval, Carole's father, was also there and for the whole week was one of the drivers. Bob's daughter Nina, who lives in Paris, arrived in the afternoon and prepared a fine meal for the veterans and members of Deep Respect.

The local paper, *La Renaissance du Bessin*, published a good article in its issue of Tuesday, May 31st, including the week's schedule. Several posters in the region brought the plans of this important week to the attention

*This is the untranslated French name, which uses quotation marks for the English words. This report is redacted from the original translation, courtesy of Association "Deep Respect."

of the public. Details of the final program could only be announced a fortnight prior to the 4th of June, because the authorities waited until the final countdown before giving their permission for some events.

After a good sleep and a very good breakfast, the group walked from the villa to the Frank Peregory monument, where the first ceremony took place. The national anthems were played, and the people of Grandcamp-Maisy heard for the first time the British anthem at a ceremonial occasion.

The group went by car to the next ceremony in front of the Rangers monument near the city hall. Both ceremonies were solemn and not too long. It was an honour for Deep Respect that Député Jean-Marc Lefranc joined the mayor of Grandcamp-Maisy and his aldermen during the ceremonies. The morning finished with a usual *vin d'honneur* and some speeches indoors. A quick and small lunch at the villa, and the group went to Vierville-sur-Mer, home of the association. The plan was to drive into the village in jeeps, but the rain was a killjoy, so that plan was canceled.

In cooperation with Association "Les Passerelles d'Omaha,"* there was a meet-and-greet with the public in an army tent behind the Omaha D-Day Museum in Vierville-sur-Mer. The posters and the articles in the papers did their job well, and the public came in numbers. The mayor of Vierville-sur-Mer welcomed the veterans and the meet-and-greet began. Each veteran received a portfolio with photos, map, and a description of his campaign during the war. The public and the press were surprised at the impressive store of information collected by Deep Respect. Compliments on all sides! The association had some income by selling drinks and homemade pies (brought by members and volunteers). Several new members announced themselves and declared ready to help the association in future. The meeting was a great success and ended with a visit to the museum.

The next ceremony in Vierville-sur-Mer was at 5:30 p.m. in front of the monument to the U.S. National Guard. The mayor of Vierville-sur-Mer, Jean-Marie Oxéant, and Député Lefranc spoke to the gathering and presented David Nelson, in absentia, with the medal of Chevalier de la Légion d'honneur (awarded on request of Deep Respect). It was an emotional ceremony, tears shed by attendees and veterans alike. Deep Respect planned to contact the embassy or the nearest French consulate to give David the medal.

Association "Les Passerelles d'Omaha" invited the whole group to have

---

*The beach bridges *(passerelles)* of Omaha Beach allowed supplies and reinforcements to be brought in from the ships. One of these is now restored.

dinner with them, and during the vin d'honneur the mayor appointed each veteran Citizen of Honour of Vierville-sur-Mer. The dinner was great and ended late. Cyril sang songs and showed again his talent as an entertainer. The group went satisfied to bed, to prepare themselves for another exciting day, the 6th of June.

The day began again with a heavy breakfast, and at 10:15 a.m., a little bit late, the cortège went to the 67th anniversary commemoration of the battle and the ceremonial reopening and rededication of Pointe du Hoc. Deep Respect had obtained invitations from the American Battle Monuments Commission for all the vets. It was an emotional and proper ceremony, with speeches from Charles Rivkin, U.S. ambassador to France, other dignitaries, and Senator Max Cleland, Vietnam veteran and secretary of the American Battle Monuments Commission. The American veterans also met U.S. Senator John Kerry. Steve Kellman and Charles Shay were special guests, and there was a symbolic empty chair for David Nelson. The British vets had their seats near the stage.

Lunch was at the restaurant La Plage d'Or, situated almost on the beach of the former "Bloody Omaha" in Vierville-sur-Mer. Then an hour's ride to the British section, where in Hermanville-sur-Mer the British Royal Navy was commemorated. All guests of Deep Respect were again in the first row during the ceremony, and again there was a vin d'honneur!

Back in Vierville-sur-Mer, there was the ceremony at 6 p.m., where the veterans laid flowers in memory of the victims on Omaha Beach. Mayor Oxéant gave the vets a special medal in the name of the village. Emotions again!

Two journalists came to the villa in the evening to interview the vets. After dinner, Eric, Bob, Cyril, Dick, Charles, and Steve spoke a long time about the emotional events of the last two days.

Tuesday, the day started again with an extensive breakfast, and journalist Monique of *La Renaisance* joined the group, along with photographer Ian Patrick and his wife, Véronique. There was a photo session with the veterans on the beach after breakfast.

Carole and Tenno had planned a quiet Tuesday for the vets, without ceremonies, and accompanied them to Isigny-sur-Mer. The group had lunch on a terrace in the center of town, followed by a drive to Bayeux to visit the British cemetery. All veterans laid red roses with a memory card in front of the headstones. Dick had recovered several victims from HMS *Isis* and wanted more flowers, because he remembered the moment the *Isis* went down, when his ship was nearby, and several survivors came on board. Deep Respect will lay flowers in the following weeks on the graves of sailors of HMS *Isis*.

The next visit was to Colleville-sur-Mer, to the Normandy American Cemetery and Memorial, were the veterans assisted the superintendent Hans Hooker in lowering the Stars and Stripes. Still a ceremony on a quiet day! Assistance in lowering a second flag was refused; Charles and Steve laid red roses for their old friends. The six veterans laid flowers that day on forty graves.

Dinner was at the restaurant Byin T-cheu Mei in Formigny, the village where the U.S. 2nd Division began its campaign and took up position between the 29th and the U.S. 1st Infantry Division.

Wednesday was exciting for Carole and Tenno: Deep Respect's first commemorative plaque. It had taken several months of preparation to get the plaque for the crew members of the 18th Minesweeping Flotilla mounted on the wall near the entrance of the Arromanches 360 circular theater, venue of the film, *The Price of Freedom*. The plaque was unveiled by Cyril, Dick, and Bob of HMS *Ready*, in the presence of sixty students from South Wilts Grammar School of Salisbury, the conseiller général Jean-Pierre Richard, the mayor of Arromanches-les-Bains Patrick Jardin, the film director Jean-Christophe Lefranc, journalists of the local press, and a lot of spectators. The ceremony began with a speech by Jean-Pierre Richard and Tenno Dogger. After the ceremony there was a vin d'honneur in the lobby of the theater.

At noon there was the departure of Steve, who had to catch a plane in Paris in the evening, because he wanted to join his granddaughter, who was graduating on Thursday. A member of Deep Respect, Odin Downey, delivered him in time to Charles de Gaulle Airport.

After lunch in Arromanches, the group had some time off to buy souvenirs and enjoy the village. In the museum there was a special reception guided by Eric Rackham, a veteran of D-Day. In his inimitable way, he explained the models of "Mulberry harbours" (portable temporary harbors) on display. Eric found on the museum wall a photo from 1944, where he can be seen with his "Duck," a large amphibious vehicle.

In the museum library, Bob presented his fine, wooden memorial plaque that shows all the emblems and names of the minesweepers of the 18th Flotilla of 1944. Cyril presented the book entitled, *They Led the Way*, by Jack Williams, founder of the Algerines Association. The book was in a special box and signed by the author, the surviving crew members, and the new chairman of the association, Malcolm Stephenson. The veterans received a bronze medal from Eric, who represented the director of the museum.

On the way back to the villa, the group stopped at Saint-Laurent-sur-Mer to visit the Maison de La Liberation, the first house with French citizens to be liberated on D-Day. Owner Sebastien Olard offered an excellent cider. After dinner at the villa, the men talked a long time about this day.

Thursday the 9th of June was a quiet day. No ceremonies planned, only some visits and sightseeing. The group started with a return to the Rangers Museum in Grandcamp-Maisy, and all signed the guest book again. After some shopping for lunch, they went to Sainte-Marguerite-d'Elle, where Eric's daughter Kaye lives. It was nice to have the lunch there. From Kaye's, the group went to Molay-Littry to see the monument to the airfield built for Operation Cobra. General de Gaulle, General Eisenhower, and Prime Minister Churchill eventually landed on that airfield.

Then there was a little surprise in Tour-en-Bessin. Sixty-seven years after Charles Shay stayed for one day in this village on 9 June 1944, the veterans visited the school, where Charles was received as one of the liberators of Tour-en-Bessin. The students and their teachers were very happy with this unexpected visit.

After seeing the city center of Bayeux, the company went to the Big Red One Assault Museum in Colleville-sur-Mer. An warm reception and presentation by the owner, again a visitors' book to sign, photos, and a good cider.

Dinner was prepared by Caroline at the villa. She made an excellent meal with a good chicken soup and boeuf bourguignon with rice. The dinner was served by Gloria and Koos.

On Friday the American section near Utah Beach had its turn. The group started with a visit to Dead Man's Corner Museum, where the vets were surprised at the wide variety of military artifacts for sale in the shop.

After a short drive, the vets arrived for lunch at Le Roosevelt, a cosy restaurant, where they were invited to sign the wall. Cyril had already signed in 2010. Photos were taken of the vets gathered behind the counter.

After a walk along the monuments and the dunes, they went to Foucarville, where a monument recalls the relative luxury of the Allied POW camp. German prisoners there were spoiled by the Americans, in contrast with the awful camps in Germany during the war. In the Foucarville camp the German POWs had a railway, a swimming pool, a theater, sports accommodations, and more than enough to eat.

In Sainte-Mère-Eglise there was a long visit to the church. On the way back to Grandcamp-Maisy, the group had a stop in Carentan, where Eric saw a "Duck" again. The owner of a military shop had recently bought it for restoration. Eric couldn't get into the Duck, as there was no ladder available.

The farewell dinner was back at La Plage d'Or in Vierville-sur-Mer. Cyril, Bob, Dick, Charles, Lucien, Eric and Gloria, Carole and Tenno, in company with Serge Letort and his wife, Geneviève, enjoyed the excellent meal with background music from the forties. With some speeches and songs, the dinner party ended, and everyone was very enthusiastic about the week's events, how they had been planned and the way they had unfolded. The veterans are looking forward to the next meeting in 2012!

Tribute to Carole Duval, Secretary, Association "Deep Respect"

by Charles Norman Shay

On behalf of David Nelson Sr. and his family, I would like to pay tribute to Carole Duval, secretary of Association "Deep Respect." Through an unyielding effort of writing letters and exchanging correspondence with government officials concerned with the approval of recipients of the prestigious medal of Chevalier de la Légion d'honneur de France, Carole was alone responsible for making it possible for David to receive this honor before he passed away on 23 July 2011.

Carole first made the acquaintance of David at the reunion of the 1st Infantry Division, when it was held at San Antonio in August of 2010. Upon learning from David that he had never been honored with this medal, Carole began her work immediately upon returning to France. Her efforts met with success when after many months she was informed that David had been approved as a recipient of the prestigious award, and it had been arranged that he would receive his medal on the beaches of Omaha, on the occasion of his first visit to Omaha since his landing on 6 June 1944. Unfortunately, this was not to be. David became seriously ill shortly before he was to depart with his son David Jr. Upon hearing the very sad news, Carole made arrangements to travel to his home in Pensacola, Florida, and presented him with the medal in the presence of his wife and family on 14 July 2011. On Sunday, 17 July, David went into a coma and departed this world on 23 July 2011. May God and the spirits be with him.

IN SPECIAL INTEREST OF REGIMENTAL CONTINUITY
TRADITIONS AND ESPRIT DE CORPS
BY ORDER OF THE SECRETARY OF THE ARMY

CAROLE DUVAL

IS DESIGNATED TO BE AN
HONORARY MEMBER
OF THE
16TH INFANTRY
REGIMENT

SIGNED
WALTER WOUDAKOSKI
MAJOR GENERAL USA
CHIEF OF INFANTRY

TRANSCRIBED FROM THE ORIGINAL DOCUMENT.

CHARLES SHAY NOMINATED MS. DUVAL FOR HONORARY MEMBERSHIP OF THE REGIMENT (HMOR). FROM LEFT: CHARLES SHAY, RAY LAMBERT, BILL RYAN, CHLOE (DAUGHTER OF CAROLE DUVAL), GEORGE HENGII, CAROLE DUVAL (IN FRONT).

V

Wounded Warrior Experience

Invited Talk
by
Charles Norman Shay

VICTORY FEATHER BY ENOCH KELLY HANEY

LOOK CLOSELY AND YOU WILL NOTICE THAT THE IMAGE OF THE SOLDIER IS TRANSFORMED IN TO A NATIVE AMERICAN WARRIOR. LARGE NUMBERS OF NATIVE AMERICANS HAVE SERVED THEIR COUNTRY IN EVERY WAR AMERICA HAS FOUGHT, NEVER LOSING SIGHT OF THEIR TRIBAL HERITAGE AND IDENTITY. MANY OF THESE WARRIORS WHO HAVE ANSWERED AMERICA'S CALL TO BATTLE HAVE DISTINGUISHED THEMSELVES WITH VALOR BEYOND THE CALL OF DUTY. *VICTORY FEATHER* IS A TRIBUTE TO ALL AMERICANS WHO HAVE VALIANTLY SERVED AND TO THOSE WHO HAVE FALLEN. A SEMINOLE/CREEK INDIAN, HANEY STRIVES TO REMAIN FAITHFUL TO HIS HERITAGE, MERGING THE PAST WITH THE PRESENT ON CANVASS AND IN BRONZE. AMONG HIS DIPLOMAS AND AWARDS, THE ARTIST HOLDS AN HONORARY DOCTOR OF LAWS FROM OKLAHOMA CITY UNIVERSITY IN 1993.

Charles Shay gave the following address* at the American Veterans Center 14th Annual Conference and Awards Gala, Washington, DC, and at The National American Indian Heritage Month Observance, Fort Stewart, Hinesvsille, Georgia.

As a Penobscot Indian elder from Indian Island, Maine, I thank the organizers of this conference for inviting me to speak to you. In my presentation, I will briefly comment on my experiences while serving with the 16th Infantry Regiment, 1st Infantry Division, as a combat medic on Omaha Beach on 6 June 1944. I will then bring my presentation to a close by relating my experiences with the 7th Infantry Regiment, 3rd Infantry Division, also as a combat medic, in North and South Korea, 1950 to 1951.

I grew up on a small Indian reservation, a small island in the Penobscot River. We called our homeland Wabanakik or Land of the Rising Sun. European settlers who arrived in northeast America over four hundred years ago colonized it and named it New England. My ancestors fought many wars in defense of our traditional hunting and fishing territories but were outgunned and outnumbered. By the time of the American Revolution, they desperately held on to a small but important part of our once vast woodland domains. This became our tribal reservation about two centuries ago. By then my nation had been reduced to about five hundred people—men, women and children, and many thought we would become extinct. White people talked about the "vanishing Indian." But we are still here.

I will now give a short resumé of my experiences during WWII. I was drafted soon after graduation from high school. Although my parents were American patriots, they objected to their sons being drafted by the military, because Indians living on the Penobscot tribal reservation were not allowed to vote. But it was wartime, and so we served. After completing basic training at Camp Pickett at Blackstone, Virginia, in the summer of 1943,

*This talk is based on my own memories as well as many military historical and geographical details concerning my experiences in WWII and the Korean War, as researched by Dr. Harald E. L. Prins, University Distinguished Professor at Kansas State University. A more extensive version of this narrative will be published in several chapters of his biography about me, titled *From Indian Island to Omaha Beach: The Story of Charles Shay, Penobscot Indian War Hero*, coauthored with his wife, Bunny McBride.

I was sent to Fort Benjamin Harrison for training as a surgical technician and finished this training by early fall of the same year. Like thousands of other American soldiers, I sailed aboard the Queen Elizabeth to England, where I joined the 2nd Medical Battalion, 16th Infantry Regiment, 1st Infantry Division, famously known as the Big Red One.

As a nineteen-year-old private, I served under Sgt. Ray Lambert, a brave combat medic, who had already participated in the North African and the Sicilian campaigns. He became my mentor, and in the past few years we have met again. I am proud to say that we have become friends. I think we are the only two medics left from our medical battalion.

After many months of training, we boarded troop transport ships that carried us across the English Channel on the night of 5 June. Soon after midnight, we anchored about twelve miles off the Normandy coast. Before dawn, we climbed down the rope ladders into the small landing craft. The sea was turbulent. At 5:00 a.m. the first wave of assault troops headed towards Omaha Beach. I served as first-aid man in Fox Company, which together with Easy Company spearheaded the invasion launched by the Big Red One. We entered hell. Many of us had never been in combat, and the sea soon turned into a bloodbath.

Once the ramps went down, it was every man for himself; one could not expect help from anyone in this situation. Landing in water almost up to

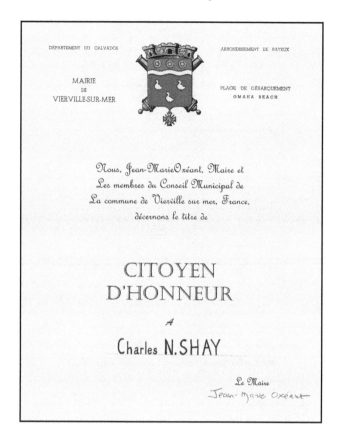

DÉPARTEMENT DU CALVADOS

ARRONDISSEMENT DE BAYEUX

MAIRIE
DE
VIERVILLE-SUR-MER

PLAGE DE DÉBARQUEMENT
OMAHA BEACH

Nous, Jean-Marie Oréant, Maire et
Les membres du Conseil Municipal de
La commune de Vierville sur mer, France,
décernons le titre de

CITOYEN
D'HONNEUR

A

Charles **N. SHAY**

Le Maire
Jean-Marie Oxéant

our chests when leaving the landing craft, many men were instantly killed or wounded because of enemy machinegun, small-arms, and mortar fire. I cannot really describe the horror, and words cannot do justice to the suffering, the heroism, the chaos on that beach. So many young men died a horrible death or were severely wounded. I survived, I believe, because of the spiritual power of my mother's prayers.

Our regiment, especially the 2nd Battalion, suffered very high casualties in wounded and dead that day. All the officers in my own company were either dead or wounded by noon. Most of the sergeants were also wounded or killed. Effectively, Fox Company had ceased to exist as a military unit. As for me, I just did my work as a combat medic, trying to rescue as many wounded men as I could on that beach. I have no idea how many men I pulled from the rising tide, how many I treated, how many I saw dying or dead. I do not know whether they formed a part of my own division or the 29th, which was mixed up with our troops. It did not matter. All that mattered was whether they would live or die.

Although there were still a few pockets of stubborn resistance, a

Proclamation #2011-10

MAYORAL PROCLAMATION

National American Indian Heritage Month Observance
November 22, 2011

WHEREAS: National American Indian Heritage Month Observance is a month proclaimed each year by the United States President to commemorate the contributions, achievements, and culture of Native Americans and Native Alaskans; and

WHEREAS: The month-long national recognition of Native Americans began in 1990 when President George H.W. Bush signed a joint congressional resolution designating November as National Native American Heritage Month. Since then, the title has expanded to celebrate the heritage, history, art, and traditions of Native Americans and Alaska Natives; and

WHEREAS: Native Americans and Native Alaskans boast a proud tradition of serving honorably and with distinction in the Armed Forces; and

WHEREAS: Fort Stewart and the Third Infantry Division is committed to recognizing the service, honor, and respect for Native Americans and Alaskans that strengthen our cultures and communities; and

WHEREAS: The sponsoring unit for the National American Indian Heritage Month observance is the Fort Stewart Medical Activity and the guest speaker is a former Third Infantry Division soldier assigned to the Medical Company of the 7th Regiment in 1950, Master Sergeant (Retired) Charles Norman Shay; and

WHEREAS: Mr. Charles Shay was one of more than 500 North American Indian soldiers who landed on the beaches of Normandy on 6 June 1944 while serving in the 1st Infantry Division, the Big Red One, as a combat medic; and

WHEREAS: Armed with only his two satchels of medical supplies, he sought refuge behind a sand dune where he tended to those who were mortally wounded and with utter disregard for his own safety, he braved a barrage of fire to pull wounded soldiers to the shelter of a sand dune where he treated them. His heroic actions that morning earned him the Silver Star; and

WHEREAS: Mr. Charles Shay earned numerous awards and receives recognition for his contributions to the United States of America as a soldier and citizen.

NOW, THEREFORE, I, James Thomas, Jr., Mayor of the City of Hinesville, do hereby pay tribute to:

Master Sergeant (Retired) Charles Norman Shay

for his valor on the battlefield and join the Third Infantry Division and others throughout the world to honor his outstanding service to our nation.

IN WITNESS WHEREOF, I have hereunto set my hand and caused the great Seal of the City of Hinesville to be affixed this 22nd day of November in the year of our Lord Two Thousand and Eleven and in the year of our City One Hundred Seventy-Four.

Attest:

Kenneth Howard, Assistant City Manager

James Thomas, Jr., Mayor
City of Hinesville

beachhead was secured by evening. Among the brave soldiers coming ashore that day, on the same stretch of beach where I had landed, was another Penobscot, a distant cousin of mine from Indian Island, Melvin Neptune. He was a scout in the 26th Regiment and had already fought in North Africa and Sicily. We briefly met in England, just before the invasion, but I never saw him again during the war.

My company was rebuilt with replacement troops, and I continued as a combat medic throughout the Normandy campaign all the way to Aachen, then the Hürtgen Forest, onwards to the Ardennes, where the Battle of the Bulge was won. In March 1945, after crossing the Rhine River near the Remagen Bridge, I was captured and taken to a *stalag* in the Ruhr Pocket.

After liberation, I returned home. The war was over, but there were few employment opportunities. So, like many others, including several other Penobscots from my reservation, I enlisted again. I briefly returned to Germany and then joined a military police battalion stationed in Vienna, Austria, where I fell in love and married a beautiful Austrian woman. By then, I had been promoted to corporal. In the summer of 1950, soon after our wedding, the Korean War broke out.

I was reassigned to the medical detachment of the 7th Infantry Regiment,

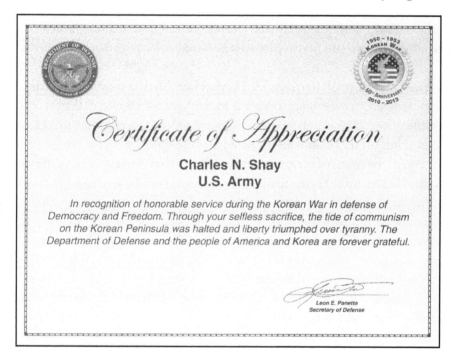

Certificate of Appreciation

Charles N. Shay
U.S. Army

In recognition of honorable service during the Korean War in defense of Democracy and Freedom. Through your selfless sacrifice, the tide of communism on the Korean Peninsula was halted and liberty triumphed over tyranny. The Department of Defense and the people of America and Korea are forever grateful.

Leon E. Panetta
Secretary of Defense

3rd Infantry Division, then stationed at Fort Devens, Massachusetts. After a brief visit to family and friends on the Penobscot reservation, it was time to leave again.

By mid September 1950, I had crossed the Pacific and landed at the Japanese island of Kyushu. We went into bivouac in the mountains of the island to prepare for our combat mission on the Korean peninsula. Soon after our arrival, I was promoted to assistant platoon sergeant and was put in charge of the litter brigade. Many of the litter bearers were young Korean men, few of whom spoke any English.

After two months, we received orders to break camp and prepare to move out, destination unknown. Boarding troopships, our regiment crossed the Sea of Japan and came ashore at Wonsan, a recently captured port city in North Korea. It was mid November, and the weather was turning bitter cold. Our mission was to set up a perimeter to guard the expanding beachhead from Wonsan to Hungnam, while the Marines were pushing into the North Korean highlands, and march to the Chinese border.

Meanwhile, South Korean troops had already captured North Korea's capital city, Pyongyang. With their Communist allies quickly losing ground and being overrun, the Chinese sent about three hundred thousand lightly armed foot soldiers into North Korea. They secretly crossed the Yalu River by night and quietly moved deep into the mountainous interior and prepared to drive the South Koreans and their UN allies back.

In Korea the Communist enemy did not fight according to the international rules of the Geneva Conference. Medics wearing red crosses were targeted, so we were ordered to remove all signs of this type of identification. Like other medics, I was armed with a carbine and a small medical kit. Other medics also carried a .45 pistol.

Few of the privates in our medical company had been in combat before. So, we had to train them, telling them: When you hear a call for medic! medic! first check with your infantry squad leader or platoon leader to verify where the wounded GI is located. If needed, ask for covering fire. Keep your head low, and if necessary, crawl low and fast. Make sure your comrades know where you are. Never leave your carbine or whatever you carry behind, and use it if necessary.

We warned them: Any wounded GI left behind may be captured, perhaps tortured for information! Those too weak to walk for hundreds of miles to a distant prison camp will be shot on the spot and stripped of shoes and clothes. And the enemy will treat captured medics exactly the same way as any combatant!

Like other medics on the front line, we had trained to carry the wounded on our backs if necessary and to carry the more seriously wounded victims by litter. Almost always, stopping loss of blood was a crucial factor to keep the wounded GI alive. So it was always important to get them as quickly as possible to our battalion aid station. That was usually a large green Army tent protected by sandbags, but we sometimes used an abandoned Korean peasant house. Whatever it was, the station was usually located not far behind our infantry in their foxholes.

As medics, we often did our work when there was a great deal of heavy firing into our positions, and we ran a serious risk of becoming casualties ourselves. Some medics stumbled into our own battalion's machinegun firing lane. Because we were not visibly marked as medics, we could easily be hit by friendly fire in the fog of war.

By late November, at least four medics in our regiment had been severely wounded on the front, five were missing in action and presumed dead, and one was captured. This was all within one week, not including an unknown number of Korean litter bearers. There would be many more casualties.

When the Marines, including my cousin, were ordered to march beyond the Chosin Reservoir, the troops risked encirclement. This is exactly what happened in late November, when the Chinese assault began with night attacks. Among the casualties were quite a few American Indians, including several Passamaquoddy from my home state. One of them was captured and another killed.

Our regiment also soon came under attack. Snow had fallen, and the cold front from Siberia plunged the temperatures to as low as −37 degrees centigrade. In the bitter cold, trench foot became a big problem, when men were not able to keep their feet warm and dry. We medics always had to check feet for frostbite and wounds.

After our forced withdrawal from North Korea, with my battalion among the very last to leave Hungnam harbor, we boarded a troopship on Christmas Eve amidst enormous explosions. We had lost many good men. The Chinese and North Korean counteroffensive across the 38th parallel after Christmas had triggered a colossal humanitarian crisis, as tens of thousands of terrified civilians were caught between two enormous armies about to crash into each other. Evacuating their ancestral towns, villages, and farms in freezing weather, masses jammed the snowy roads in search of food, shelter, and clothing assistance. Fleeing south, a miserable crowd of cold and hungry refugees tried to reach the UN defense line. Our military continued recruiting South Korean laborers—and there were plenty of them among the displaced, hungry masses—training them as backup litter squads.

With enormous artillery and air strikes bombing and dropping napalm on the enemy, Operation Thunderbolt was launched in late January 1951. The strategic objective of this UN counteroffensive was simple: Destroy or capture all Communist enemies south of the Han River, then firmly in Chinese hands. American fighter planes strafed, bombed and dropped napalm on what appeared to be columns of enemy troops moving along snow-covered roads deep below, but also caused horrendous carnage among the refugees.

In early February, we no longer saw rotting bodies and no more live refugees. We were back in combat. One knows that war is hell when dawn comes on your frontline position, and one looks out and sees hundreds of dead from the previous night attack by hundreds of screaming, wild Chinese and North Koreans, who had no regard for life. Some of our medics became traumatized by the deafening noise of deadly explosions in the killing fields. One shell-shocked medic in my regiment, a litter squad leader like me, became such an emotional wreck that he ended up in a hospital in Japan for recovery. When I later heard about this case, I felt sympathetic, as this incident reminded me of my own brief emotional breakdown on the German front line in the dreadful Hürtgen Forest in late 1944.

Promoted to platoon sergeant, I was now the senior noncommissioned officer at our 2nd Battalion aid station. As the sergeant in charge of the two dozen litter bearers in our medical platoon, I was always in close touch with Captain Gilbert Campbell, a young medical doctor in charge of our battalion aid station. To kill time, usually between battles and when not on the move, we often played cards for fun.

It was bitter cold, with 40 mph winds driving sheets of snow all over the place. Our infantry squads trooped up and down the hills through snow drifts, and almost blinded by the storm. Fighting in mountainous terrain just a few miles south of the Han River, we ran into problems evacuating our wounded along the slippery snow and ice trails down to the litter jeeps on the dirt roads below. In this rugged and often icy terrain, it took four and sometimes six men per litter.

During combat, we kept our two-way radio within reach, in or just outside the camouflaged and sand-bagged tent or hut serving as our first-aid station. This allowed us to remain in contact with commanders equipped with walkie-talkies, when they radioed in for medical assistance. That is how I received orders to direct my litter teams, strong young South Korean men, few of whom spoke any English, to wherever the seriously wounded men were waiting for evacuation. Of course we all knew that a wounded GI left behind was doomed to die.

On the front, everyone in the medical platoon, doctor and litter carrier alike, was vulnerable to direct small-arms fire and shelling by 120 and 82 mm mortar. Of course, as combat medics we had to risk our own lives to rescue wounded from the battlefield. However, not all our own troops were killed or wounded by enemy fire, as friendly-fire accidents were an ongoing problem.

On a freezing cold day, 16 February, platoons in our battalion charged a Chinese stronghold on a high ridge near Chonyon-ni and the ancient walled city of Sansong-ni. From this location, marked as Hill 287 on UN military maps, the enemy controlled an important road juncture. In this attack, we suffered many casualties. Among them was a combat medic, a WWII veteran from a small town in Texas, killed in a barrage of mortar fire after jumping from a foxhole to rescue a fallen soldier crying out for help. In this combat operation, I also sprang into action, directing my litter bearers to the terrible carnage under deafening fire, trying to rescue as many wounded comrades as we could. This is where I was awarded a Bronze Star, the first of three I received in the Korean War.

In late April, the Chinese and their North Korean allies prepared for a huge counteroffensive. Their generals could tap into a seemingly endless reservoir of human resources—poor peasant soldiers. Poorly fed. Poorly dressed and poorly armed, they were just cannon fodder. On the night of 22 April, after a two-hour artillery barrage, almost 350,000 Chinese and North Korean soldiers stormed towards the UN military outposts and forward positions, by midnight and under a full moon. As usual, they came in waves, running, shooting and screaming. Soon we had our hands full with wounded and dying. Running up and down the slopes, our litter squads struggled to carry them as quickly as they could to the battalion aid stations and regimental collecting station.

As one battalion surgeon in my regiment later recalled, the influx of wounded GIs was so overwhelming that it was impossible to do anything other than to tie on a tag with name, rank, date, time, and type of injury. The casualties were unloaded onto a field in front of the collecting station by the scores. Our efforts as medics with such a mass of casualties was to triage for visible bleeding, check the pulse and blood pressure. After fierce close-in fighting until dawn, often with bloodied bayonet, our troops piled up Chinese corpses like cordwood in front of their positions. One could look down the hillside for miles and see nothing but Chinese bodies.

On a mountain slope the morning of 25 April, I had two fellow medics from my platoon climbing up and down Hill 289 in search of wounded GIs. Suddenly an excited Korean peasant ran up to us, and I quickly turned to one of my English-speaking Korean litter bearers for translation. That is how I found out a suspicious stranger was hiding in the nearby village. Armed with my carbine, I found a Chinese soldier, probably a scared deserter, and took him as captive. I was later told that this was our division's first captive in this three-day counteroffensive.

Master Sergeant Charles Norman Shay

*Is Granted and Assigned
the Distinction of*

𝕯𝖎𝖘𝖙𝖎𝖓𝖌𝖚𝖎𝖘𝖍𝖊𝖉 𝕸𝖊𝖒𝖇𝖊𝖗
𝖔𝖋 𝖙𝖍𝖊
𝖀𝖓𝖎𝖙𝖊𝖉 𝕾𝖙𝖆𝖙𝖊𝖘 𝕬𝖗𝖒𝖞
𝕸𝖊𝖉𝖎𝖈𝖆𝖑 𝕯𝖊𝖕𝖆𝖗𝖙𝖒𝖊𝖓𝖙 𝕽𝖊𝖌𝖎𝖒𝖊𝖓𝖙

*This Appointment Recognizes His Contributions
to Regimental Continuity,
Tradition, and Esprit de Corps*

BY ORDER OF THE SURGEON GENERAL

ERIC B. SCHOOMAKER
Lieutenant General
The Surgeon General

OTSG Form 520-2, 1 May 89

In early June, we crossed the Hantan River and prepared for our final assault, driving the Communists back north, across the 38th parallel. Our task was the capture of the Iron Triangle in the heart of the Korean peninsula. Within a week, suffering many casualties again, our regiment had fought its way to Chorwon, a ruined town in the Iron Triangle. Our regiment suffered serious casualties, with well over two hundred GIs wounded and more than forty killed. Among our medics at least five were wounded and two killed, one by sniper fire. Numbed by the sight and smell of hundreds of dead, dying and mangled humans, I was becoming depressed by the misery of war.

On 14 June, our entire medical company, now headed by Major Jensen, assembled near the 7th Regiment's temporary headquarters. This is when I

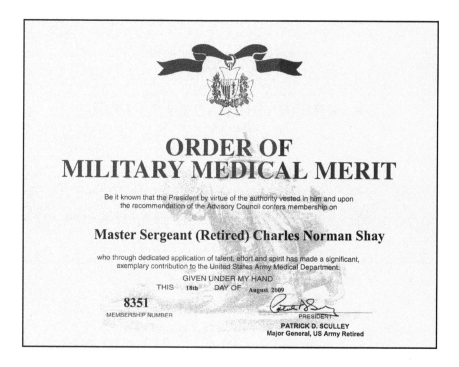

received a star on top of my combat medical badge, signifying that it was my second wartime award. Ten days later, I was promoted to sergeant first class.

With about one million enemy soldiers killed or wounded and the Communist armies driven from South Korean territory, the war had now reached its first terrible anniversary. But with about four million young Chinese left for the meat grinder, the prospect of endless battles for hilltop positions was dreadful. And so it was that the UN passed a resolution to end hostilities on 28 June, with negotiations for restoration of the prewar political boundaries beginning in early July.

With diplomats now talking, soldiers continued to bleed, keeping us medics busy. More fighting lay ahead. During the battle of the Sobang Hills in the center of the Iron Triangle, in the first week of July, I led our litter teams up and down the slopes. Exposed to deadly enemy small arms, automatic weapons, and grenade barrages, we carried the casualties back to the aid station for treatment and evacuation. On the second day of fierce combat, I found myself promoted to master sergeant on the spot. I took the position of Jack Cobb, who had just been awarded a battlefield commission as second lieutenant.

Fierce fighting along the slopes, peaks and valleys of this stubbornly

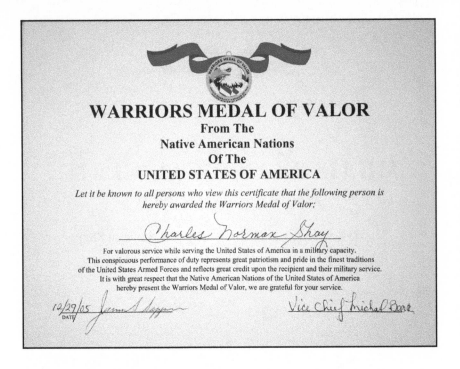

defended high ground continued for three or four days, and many hundreds of dead Chinese were left behind, their bodies decomposing quickly in the sweltering heat. Because the litter jeeps driving across the only accessible road had come under enemy fire and had to wait at a distance, our litter squads had to walk long distances across this rough terrain. For a few most critically wounded soldiers, our division's bubble chopper was called in by radio, to be rushed to a MASH unit. When the four-day battle for the Sobang Hills was over, we returned to our bivouac. No one wanted to be reminded of the carnage left behind, but twenty-six of our comrades had been killed and another one hundred and seventy wounded. Among the casualties were several medics. It did not help that Chinese losses were much higher, with well over fifteen hundred casualties, about half of whom were killed.

Our 2nd Battalion was officially commended with a unit citation, noting that the troops displayed "extraordinary heroism of duty and extraordinary heroism in action against the enemy" at Hill 717. I myself was again personally recognized for what they call "heroic altruism," administering "medical aid to the stricken soldiers" under deadly enemy fire. This time I was awarded a second oak leaf cluster to my bronze battle star.

With the Chinese driven from the Sobang Hills, most of the Iron Triangle was now under UN control, and a stalemate had been reached along a new line of demarcation north of the 38th parallel, which the UN referred to as the "main line of resistance" (MLR). But the fighting continued, with frequent clashes over key mountains, hills and ridges all along the unstable front. By now I was growing weary of war, and I was eager to leave Korea. Many of my old comrades, with whom I had shared so much hardship, boredom, pain, and laughter since leaving Fort Devens in Massachusetts, were no longer in our medical company—some had been reassigned, others had been killed, and many were wounded and evacuated, never to be heard from again. One day Captain Campbell also packed his duffel bag. I was happy for this brave young medical doctor returning home, alive and well, with several medals, including the Purple Heart.

Meanwhile, the heavy summer rains continued, turning clothes damp and paths into slippery mud. I was counting the days when I could go back to Indian Island. That day finally came in November 1951, after a full year in Korea. A few weeks later, just before Christmas, I was home, safe, back with my family and never looked back—until recently, when people began asking me to share my personal story. Ladies and gentlemen, I thank you for your listening to my story and say *woliwon*, a word in my own language, which means farewell.

ON INDIAN ISLAND, "THIS MEMORIAL IS DEDICATED TO ALL NATIVE AMERICAN WARRIORS, ESPECIALLY WABANAKI WARRIORS: PENOBSCOT, PASSAMAQUODDY, MALISEET, MICMAC." SCULPTED BY TIM SHAY, COMMISSIONED BY THE AUTHOR.

VI

Native American Veterans Day

State of Maine
June 21

State seal: *Dirigo*, I Lead. The State of Maine leads
the nation by signing into law Maine's Native
American Veterans Day

FIRST NATIVE AMERICAN VETERANS DAY
IN THE
HISTORY OF AMERICA

LETTER FROM DR. HARALD E. L. PRINS TO CHARLES SHAY
JUNE 21, 2009

Dear Charles,

Sixty-five years ago, Melvin Neptune, John Banks, and you were in Normandy, as were several Passamaquoddy, Maliseet, and Micmac. At least two of these brave Wabanaki warriors had already lost their lives, including a Micmac who had been taken captive and was executed. And one was later killed in the liberation of my homeland from enemy occupation and lies buried in a small grave just north of the village where our friend Gus grew up. And at least one Penobscot was wounded while helping to push the enemy back into its own territory.

Today, with the first official Native American Veterans Day marked on the official agenda of Maine, we're thinking of so many—not only those who made the ultimate sacrifice, but also all those who made it out alive. Maine leads the country, living up to its motto—*Dirigo*. And not only in this country but all of North America, indeed the entire Western Hemisphere, for there is no country in South or Central America either that honors its Native veterans.

Two years ago, when you

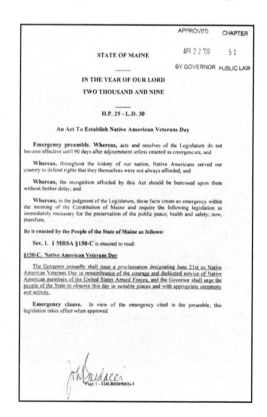

started on Project Omaha Beach, exposing your personal life history, sharing your emotional memories about horrific events you thought you had left behind you forever, a ball started rolling. And like a snowball coming down a slope, it gained size and momentum and has become a symbolic gift to fellow Native veterans, past and present, their relatives and friends, to the Wabanaki nations and far beyond.

You had a vision two years ago, when the State of Maine honored you by declaring 6 June 2007 Native American Veterans History Day, and you wanted to make that a permanent event on a day that would symbolically tie all Wabanaki veterans, including those like your brothers who fought in the Pacific or Italy and had nothing to do with the Normandy invasion. That vision has become reality with the support of wonderful people, including Donna Loring, Donald Soctomah, and so many others who dedicated their energy to helping make this happen.

As you often have reminded us, this is not about you, not about personal recognition or individual glory. Guided by the spirits, you stepped forward and others followed, because you knew that this was and is something noble, something that lifts us all—like the sun rising this morning.

First Native American Veterans Day in the history of America signed into law by Governor John E. Baldacci with Charles Shay to his right.

State of Maine

Proclamation

WHEREAS, the heroism and contributions of Native Americans in defense of the United States, especially during World War II, have been sadly overlooked; and

WHEREAS, their history has not been appropriately or thoroughly documented; and

WHEREAS, an estimated 30,000 Native Americans enlisted in the military during World War II, including at least 156 Penobscot and Passamaquoddy Indians, as well as Maliseet and Micmac Indians living in Maine; and

WHEREAS, Maine is privileged to claim as its own Charles Norman Shay, a Penobscot Indian and American hero, who served during World War II, the Korean War and Cold War; and

WHEREAS, Mr. Shay served with great distinction as a combat medic in the 16th Regiment of the First Infantry Division and landed on Omaha Beach during the first assault on D-Day, earning a Silver Star for his "unselfish heroism"; and

WHEREAS, Mr. Shay continued to fight as a member of the U.S. Army at the Battle of the Bulge and other major conflicts until he became a Prisoner of War during the drive to defeat Nazi Germany; and

WHEREAS, Mr. Shay, after liberation, continued his military career, serving as master sergeant in the Third Medical Platoon, 7th Infantry Regiment of the 3rd Infantry Division during the Korean War, earning a Bronze Star with Two Oak Leaf Clusters for Valor, and further honorably served in the U.S. Air Force for more than a decade afterwards; and

WHEREAS, Mr. Shay returned home to Maine in 2002 and is participating in a history project to help document his story and the stories of other Native Americans who have worn the uniform of the United States; and

WHEREAS, Mr. Shay seeks no recognition for himself except as it helps to bring attention to the bravery and sacrifice of other Native Americans whose service to the United States is at risk of being lost to history,

NOW, THEREFORE, I, JOHN E. BALDACCI, Governor of the State of Maine, do hereby proclaim June 6, 2007 as

NATIVE AMERICAN VETERANS HISTORY DAY

throughout the State of Maine, and urge all citizens to recognize this observance.

In testimony whereof, I have caused the Great Seal of the State to be hereunto affixed GIVEN under my hand at Augusta this thirtieth day of May in the Year of our Lord Two Thousand and Seven.

John E. Baldacci
Governor

Matthew Dunlap
Secretary of State
TRUE ATTESTED COPY

The
Silver Star
Honorable Service Medal

is presented to

MSgt Charles N. Shay

in recognition of his honorable service as a Prisoner of War during World War II and for his service in the Armed Forces of our country. WE the CITIZENS of the STATE OF MAINE, express our sincere appreciation for his courage and his willingness to serve our state and nation. We are proud of him, and grateful to him for his commitment to the defense of freedom.

Governor of Maine

Adjutant General of Maine

In Support of LD 30

A DIRECTIVE TO ESTABLISH
JUNE 21 NATIVE AMERICAN VETERANS DAY
IN THE STATE OF MAINE

Address by Charles N. Shay, 18 February 2009

Mr. Chairman and distinguished members of the Joint Standing Committee on Legal and Veterans Affairs, I am Charles Norman Shay, a tribal elder of the Penobscot Indian Nation. Standing here before you in our state Capitol, I am humbled by the thought that my father, Leo Shay, my grandfather Joseph Nicolar, and my great-great-grandfather John Neptune all served as my tribe's representatives to this legislative body.

It is an honor to appear before this committee as a Native American combat veteran of the Second World War, the Korean War, and the Cold War. As you know, not many people in the State of Maine or elsewhere across this great country are aware of the role of Native American soldiers, marines, seamen, pilots, or medics in our country's history. And fewer still may know that not every Native American veteran is a warrior who went to the battlefield to kill enemies. I myself, for example, never shot in anger or self-defense but was a combat medic dedicated to treating and trying to save the lives of wounded comrades. Also, there are Native female veterans who served in the military.

My own status as a veteran can be summed up as follows: I served in the Medical Detachment of the U.S. Armed Forces for twenty years, ending my military career as a master sergeant in 1964. Drafted as a nineteen-year-old in 1943, I was trained as a combat medic and then sent to England, where I was attached to an assault platoon in the 16th Regiment of the 1st Infantry Division.

My baptism by fire came on D-Day, when I landed on Omaha Beach at dawn. In March 1945, I became a POW but was liberated three weeks later. After the war, I returned to military service and was attached to the U.S. Military Police in occupied Austria. Promoted to Master Sergeant, I later served as a combat medic in the 7th Regiment of the 3rd Infantry Division during the Korean War. My final stint in the military was in the

6th Weather Squadron of the U.S. Air Force. For most of my many years in military uniform, I was stationed overseas: Germany, Austria, and the southern Pacific.

Although I am proud of my military record in years of war and in times of peace, my service in our country's national defense is not unique. For instance, there were perhaps as many as fifty thousand North American Indians in the military in the Second World War, including over eighty young Penobscot men and four women. Among them were my three brothers and myself. All four of us returned home alive. Many others from our tribal community were wounded but survived, and a few were killed overseas. The same is true for our Passamaquoddy, Maliseet, and Micmac neighbors in Maine and across the Canadian border.

For many centuries, these four Indian tribes have been allied in the Wabanaki Confederacy in order to defend our ancestral homelands against common enemies. On the 21st of June in 1775, just four days after the Battle of Bunker Hill, my own forefather, Chief Joseph Orono, extended his hand in friendship to leaders of the American Revolution and pledged the support of his proud warriors. Soon thereafter, the other Wabanaki tribes followed suit. Without their military role in the Revolutionary War, much of the territory now called Maine may not have become part of the United States. But our people well remember that this commitment by our ancestors was based on the recognition of respect for our traditional rights and protection of our ancestral lands.

Since the Revolutionary War, the Wabanaki tribes have provided a few thousand brave young men willing to serve in the Armed Forces of the United States or Canada. Perhaps a hundred of those Wabanakis were killed, wounded, or taken captive. And over a dozen men from our tribes found their final resting place in war cemeteries overseas.

Today, I think of them and feel sad that so many did not have the opportunity to live a long and healthy life, to marry, or to be blessed with children. All too often, all we now know about them is their names, a few dates, perhaps, and sometimes a photograph or two. We must not forget them, because their sufferings and sacrifices enable us all to enjoy our freedom.

As a Native American combat veteran who made it back from many battlefields alive and happily resides in the same Indian Island village that Chief Joseph Orono called home, I strongly support this important directive to officially establish June 21st as Native American Veterans Day in Maine.

We have chosen this particular date because it commemorates the long-standing military alliance between the Wabanaki tribes and the United States of America. Notably, this date steers clear of the national November 11th Veterans Day, making it possible for Native veterans such as myself, who do not want to separate ourselves from other American veterans, to march shoulder to shoulder in Veterans Day parades, regardless of differences in our ethnic, religious, or class backgrounds. Also marking the beginning of the summer season, June 21st is the longest day of the year and promises to become an important day of historical reflection and cultural ceremony in which we collectively honor ancestors, relatives and friends who have made personal sacrifices for our freedom.

Based on these considerations and more, I urge you to support and pass LD 30 and make June 21st a day when our people can dance, sing and rejoice to commemorate and honor our brave warriors, many of whom paid the ultimate price for the country we love and so proudly defend. By passing LD 30 our state will become the first in the Union to honor its Native population with such historic distinction. Woliwon!

ON THE SIGNING OF NATIVE AMERICAN VETERANS DAY INTO LAW BY MAINE GOVERNOR JOHN E. BALDACCI

COMMEMORATIVE ADDRESS BY CHARLES N. SHAY, SPRING 2009

As one of the last surviving Maine Indian combat veterans who served our country in the Second World War, I am grateful for the opportunity to witness Governor Baldacci sign legislation formally establishing Native American Veterans Day in Maine.

Now almost eighty-five years old, I am a tribal elder of the Penobscot Indian Nation in Maine. We are one of four tribes in our state. Together with our brothers and sisters of the Passamaquoddy, Maliseet, and Micmac, we have been allied nations in the Wabanaki Confederacy. Since the beginning of the American Revolution, our people have stood shoulder to shoulder with other Americans and Canadians in many wars, fighting common enemies.

During the past century, for example, a few dozen Wabanakis from Maine served in WWI. And about two hundred of our people volunteered or were drafted into the military during WWII. Many later served in the Korean War, the Vietnam War, and the Iraq wars.

As a veteran of WWII and the Korean War, I am not unique. My personal story has become

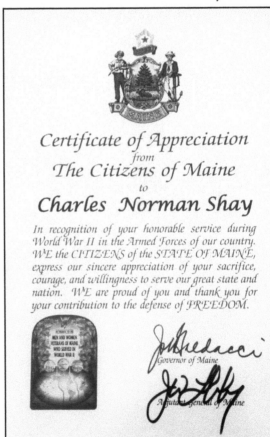

Certificate of Appreciation
from
The Citizens of Maine
to
Charles Norman Shay

In recognition of your honorable service during World War II in the Armed Forces of our country. WE the CITIZENS of the STATE OF MAINE, express our sincere appreciation of your sacrifice, courage, and willingness to serve our great state and nation. WE are proud of you and thank you for your contribution to the defense of FREEDOM.

Governor of Maine

Adjutant General of Maine

quite well known over the past few years because I agreed to step forward in the hope of drawing attention to our forgotten history, soldiers, and sacrifices.

I was baptized by fire on bloody Omaha, June 6, 1944. On that very same day, now remembered as D-Day, there were hundreds of North American Indian warriors storming German fortifications in French Normandy. Among them were another Penobscot, and also a Passamaquoddy. Both young Indian men came ashore hours after me on Omaha Beach. Meanwhile, a few Mali-

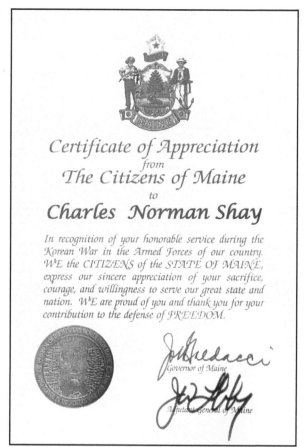

Certificate of Appreciation
from
The Citizens of Maine
to
Charles Norman Shay

In recognition of your honorable service during the Korean War in the Armed Forces of our country. WE the CITIZENS of the STATE OF MAINE, express our sincere appreciation of your sacrifice, courage, and willingness to serve our great state and nation. WE are proud of you and thank you for your contribution to the defense of FREEDOM.

Governor of Maine

Adjutant General of Maine

seet and Micmac soldiers landed on nearby Juno Beach. At least three of these brave-hearted Wabanakis were killed within the next few days of heavy fighting, including one who was first captured and then executed by the SS. Their stories have not been told, and their names and the sacrifices they made have not been remembered.

Many more were wounded and some captured. While a good number of us were decorated with Purple Hearts, Bronze and Silver Stars, when we came back to our reservations, we did not talk about our experiences. We were not asked. And so we forgot, and our country forgot—a forgetting that has become tradition.

Now, nearly sixty-five years have passed since WWII ended. Almost all of the Maine Indian veterans from my generation have now passed away, including my three brothers. Those of us still alive have few memories of that war.

As a combat medic who served in the Korean War as well as WWII,

I well know that bullets and shrapnel do not distinguish between soldiers of different racial, national, ethnic, or religious heritage. But, I also know that not all those who served and sacrificed have been—or are—treated equally. Nor are our contributions as veterans, regardless of battlefield honors, always equally remembered.

I am grateful that our state is living up to its motto—*Dirigo*: I lead—and is now the first state in the Union to formally mark a Native American Veterans Day. We have chosen June 21st as the date for this commemoration, because it was on that day in 1775 that our Wabanaki ancestors joined the American Revolution. From now on, this day will provide us with the opportunity to remind the general public, as well as our own Native communities, about Native American contributions and sacrifices to the spirit of freedom, and to honor those who have served or are now serving our country.

I am honored and grateful for this opportunity to share my thoughts and feelings about this landmark legislation. I offer these comments in memory of so many comrades who have passed away or cannot be here because of old age, poor health, or other personal reasons. I trust they are with us here in spirit. Woliwon!

State of Maine

Be it known to all that
We, the Members of the Senate and
House of Representatives,
join in recognizing

Charles Norman Shay,

of Indian Island, a Penobscot Indian who valiantly fought in World War II and the Korean War, on the occasion of his returning to Europe's battlefields to tell his stories of the war. Mr. Shay, continuing a long tradition of Native Americans fighting in all of America's wars, from the Civil War to Iraq, was a combat medic in the 16th Regiment of the 1st Infantry Division, which heroically stormed Omaha Beach in Normandy, France on June 6, 1944 and lost 1,000 men. Private Shay received the Silver Star for extraordinary valor on D-Day. He remained on the front, fighting in the Battle of the Bulge, and was captured by the Germans after crossing the Rhine Bridge at Remagen, spending the rest of the war as a prisoner-of-war until liberation. Mr. Shay returned to Indian Island in 1945, but re-enlisted in early 1946, returning to Germany. He was assigned to the Military Police in occupied Austria, where he remained for 4 years. In 1950, he joined the 3rd Infantry Division and fought in North Korea, where he was promoted to Master Sergeant and won the Bronze Star. In 1953, Mr. Shay joined the United States Air Force and participated in the atomic bomb test in the Marshall Islands, retiring in 1964. He returned to Vienna to work for the International Atomic Energy Agency for 20 years and then for 3 years as Security Officer for the Vienna Office of the United Nations High Commissioner of Refugees until 1988. At the age of 83, Mr. Shay will return for the first time to the World War II battlefields to detail the oral history in situ with video camera, sound recorder and notepad. We extend our appreciation to Mr. Shay for his extraordinary dedication and service to our Nation, and we send him our best wishes on this remarkable and valuable project he is undertaking; And be it ordered that this official expression of sentiment be sent forthwith on behalf of the 123rd Legislature and the people of the State of Maine.

HLS 542

Given this fifth day of June, 2007
at the State Capitol
Augusta, Maine

Beth Edmonds
President of the Senate

Glenn Cummings
Speaker of the House

Joy J. O'Brien
Secretary of the Senate

Millicent M. MacFarland
Clerk of the House

Introduced by: Rep. Donna M. Loring

From: the Penobscot Nation

VII

The Cape Collar

BEFORE I COME TO A CLOSE, I would like to write about a ceremonial collar that was worn by my mother, Florence Nicolar, in a photograph taken of her when she was about sixteen or seventeen years old. She was born in 1884, so this photograph dates back to approximately 1900 or 1901. I showed the photograph to James Francis, the tribal historian, and he was able to determine that this was the same collar that is on exhibit at the Smithsonian National Museum of the American Indian in a collection of Penobscot Indian artifacts. I then decided to have a replica of this ceremonial collar made for myself, because after seeing the photograph of my mother wearing this ceremonial collar, for some reason I just had to have it. Knowing that it was very intricate and difficult work to reproduce it, I had to find the right person who would be able to do it. I went through the names of people on the reservation who did such work, and finally, at the suggestion of others I talked with, settled on Jennifer Neptune, who I was told was the only person who could reproduce this very intricate piece of art. I called her down to my home and talked with her; we made an agreement on the cost of her work and the approximate number of hours she would have to invest in this project, and I commissioned her to do the work for me. This was now four years ago, in 2006, and in the spring of 2009 we had a ceremony at the tribal Community Building where the Governor, council members, and relatives were present when Jennifer presented me with the collar and placed it over my shoulders (photo opposite).

Following is an article by Jennifer Neptune about her experience in the research and production of the collar replica.

APPLIED ANTHROPOLOGY
BRINGING BACK THE PAST

Jennifer Sapiel Neptune

Near the turn of the twentieth century, a young Penobscot woman sat for a photograph, wearing a very old and elaborately beaded ceremonial chief's collar. She was the daughter of Joseph and Elizabeth Nicolar and descendent of a long line of tribal leaders. Her name was Florence Nicolar, and she would go on to live a long life, marry Leo Shay, raise a family, and be remembered as a fine basketmaker and dedicated advocate for our tribe. Her efforts brought increased educational opportunities, the right for Native people in the state of Maine to vote in state and federal elections, and the first bridge that would connect our small village of Indian Island in the Penobscot River to the mainland.

Now, over one hundred years later, the photograph has resurfaced and found its way back to her son Charles Shay. Charles brought the photograph of his mother to our tribal historian, James Francis, who recognized the collar as one he had seen in the book, *Penobscot Man*, by Frank G. Speck. James then traced it to the Penobscot collection in the National Museum of the American Indian.

In the late nineteenth century, the idea of the "vanishing Indian" took hold in anthropology, leading to a specialized field known as "salvage ethnology," which sought to save traditional knowledge, lifeways, and material culture. Collecting examples of material culture to be sold into museum collections became a business for some—which was how the collar Florence wears in the photograph came to be purchased by George Heye, sometime before 1905, becoming part of the collections of the Museum of the American Indian. I have always found it ironic that we as a people and culture did not vanish, but during this time many of our tribes' most precious material objects did.

As a teenager I spent a lot of time in the library at the University of

"Applied Anthropology" article by permission of the authors and editors of the textbook for which it was commissioned: William Haviland, Harald Prins, Bunny McBride, and Dana Walrath. *Cultural Anthropology: The Human Challenge*. Belmont, CA: Thomson Wadsworth, 2011.

Maine, looking through photographs in books of Penobscot beadwork, appliqué ribbon-work, basketry, and carvings that were by then in museums all over the world. I dreamed of being able to visit these objects, to study them up close and to be able to find a way to bring them back into our world. It was for this reason that I went into anthropology, to learn how to research and write about my own culture. I started doing reproductions of the old beadwork designs, became a basketmaker, consulted on museum exhibitions, sold my own artwork, and worked with the Maine Indian Basketmakers Alliance promoting the work of basketmakers and artists from the four tribes in Maine.

In the spring of 2006, Charles showed me the photograph of his mother and asked me if I could make a reproduction of the collar for him.

As I worked on the collar, I was struck by how much had changed since the late eighteenth century when the original collar was made. Back then the wool, silk ribbon, and beads she used had come by ship, horse, and foot from trade or treaty annuities; my materials were ordered over the Internet and arrived by UPS and FedEx. She had worked by the light of the sun or fire; I worked mostly in the evenings with electric lights. Her world had northern forests still untouched by logging and filled with caribou and wolves; my world had airplanes, cars, and motorboats.

As I worked, I thought about what had stayed the same. We had lived and watched the sun rise and set on the same Island our ancestors had for over seven thousand years. I wondered if we had stitched the same prayers into our work, if we used the same medicinal plants to soothe our aching hands and shoulders at the end of the day.

There are no words that can express how gratifying it was to hand over the finished collar to Charles and to have played a part in returning to him, his family, and our tribe a part of our history.

One hundred years ago, when the collar left my community, anthropology seemed to be about taking objects, stories, and information away. As an anthropologist and artist, I believe that I have a responsibility to use what I have learned to give back to my community. I have been so fortunate to be able to spend time in museum collections, visiting objects that most of my own people will never have the opportunity to see. What I learned from my time with the collar was that the objects that are left still have a relationship with us today; they have a story that wants to be told, and they are waiting for someone to listen.

As displayed (above and opposite) at the author's residence on Indian Island, this cape collar, beaded by Jennifer Sapiel Neptune, was recreated from an original in the collections of the National Museum of the American Indian. A historic image of Florence Nicolar Shay wearing the collar inspired Charles N. Shay, Florence's son, to commission its reproduction.

The museum text reads: "Key to the regalia of Penobscot men was the cape collar, which was worn for dances, ceremonies, inaugurations of governors and chiefs, as well as special occasions. This distinctive style was derived from the decorated great coats that were worn in the late 1700s and early 1800s. Collars were ornamented with silk ribbon work and white seed beads, which were used to create double curve motifs.

"Today Charles N. Shay, a recipient of France's National Order of the Legion of Honor and decorated World War II veteran, wears this collar for special occasions and ceremonies."

A PERSONAL LETTER FROM JENNIFER SAPIEL NEPTUNE
TO CHARLES SHAY

AUGUST 2, 2010

Dear Charles,

Sweetgrass was burned, prayers were said many times after I agreed to recreate the collar that had belonged to your family. As I sat at my kitchen table placing each stitch and bead—and now I search for the words that will convey what a humbling, inspiring, and healing experience it was.

In August of 2006, I stood awestruck in front of the original collar. I had only seen it before in black-and-white photographs. Now I could see how beautiful and complex it really was. It was powerful; it radiated energy, and it had seen so much of our people's history. I was overwhelmed; I wondered if I was in over my head. I questioned how I could ever do a reproduction that would be good enough to give back to you. But I could feel it wanted to return. It had to be made.

I remembered all that had happened that had led me to be standing in Suitland, Maryland, among the collections of the Smithsonian Institution. Over two hundred years ago, the collar had been made of broadcloth and yards of silk and thousands of beads. Old designs stitched by hand by the light of the sun and firelight, in a time when our language was spoken, before Maine was ever a state, and we still retained most of our land. A chief's collar, worn by tribal leaders through the good and the bad, until all that was left was our island. One hundred years later, your mother, Florence Nicolar Shay, would pose for a photograph wearing the collar. The collar would be collected by an anthropologist and find its way into the collections of the Smithsonian Institution. Decades would pass, life would move on, and then one day your nephew Tim Shay would find the photograph of your beautiful young mother. He would bring that photograph to you; you would bring the photograph to our tribal historian, James Francis, who would recognize the collar as one he had seen. Its location would be found; you would tell me the story, show me the photograph, and ask me to make a reproduction of it, and I would make arrangements, fly to Washington, DC, take the Métro, and walk the rest of the way to the Cultural Resources Center on one of the hottest days of the year to see it, measure it, touch it, and be awed by it.

That day I saw amazing things that had came from our tribe. I left full of emotions—elated by what I had seen, saddened by how few will get the opportunity, and excited and scared of the project I was about to take on. As I was walking past the gate, I was thinking about what a strange coincidence it was that the day I left Indian Island on this trip was August 5th, your mother's birthday. A yellow butterfly floated up and danced all around me, and I knew without a doubt that I would find a way, that there would be help, and to just have faith.

One would think finding wool in Maine would be fairly simple. One would assume that silk ribbons would also be easy to procure. It was not. I spent the rest of 2006 using the Internet to track down wool broadcloth in the right shade of red, silk ribbons of different sizes and colors, and thread to match the ribbons. Supplies came from all corners of the country.

Finally in 2007, I had all the supplies and was ready to begin. I started with the silk ribbon-work. It was humbling, to say the least. The ribbons were slippery and difficult to make into the intricate shapes that were on the collar. I had never done ribbon-work before and mistakenly thought that it would be easier than the beadwork. I was discouraged but very determined.

During the spring of 2007, I was traveling a lot for work. Sometimes I would take the collar with me to work on in the evenings. At a conference in Colorado, I walked past an antique store that just kept pulling me to go in. Finally I went in and looked around and felt drawn to the back of the store, where on the floor in a corner behind some other stuff was a sweetgrass flat basket. It was in perfect condition and was under $20. I took it back to my room, and all the ribbon, thread, needles and tools I was using on the collar fit inside. It gave me encouragement not to give up. I was going to need it soon.

In July I woke up one morning in extreme pain beyond anything I could have ever imagined. Sparing all the grisly details, what followed were days that tested my will to live. The night before I was to have surgery, I stayed awake, watching as my temperature climbed way over 100 degrees, putting the surgery at risk. As the sun rose, I went outside and burned some sweetgrass and seriously considered whether I was leaving this world or going to fight to stay in it. I really felt that morning that the choice was mine. I prayed very hard. I love my husband, my family, my friends, but what kept me from giving up that day and the days that followed was the thought that I have to finish Charlie's collar.

I spent the rest of that year and most of the next recovering and trying to be in a good frame of mind to work on the collar again. I worked on the collar on and off through 2008, dealing with big changes that were happening at work and healing from the traumas of the previous year. Finally, in 2009 things began to flow, and progress was made. I took time off from work and stitched from sunup until way past midnight.

I thought a lot about the woman who had made the original collar and what she would have seen and experienced in her life. The late eighteenth and early nineteenth century was such a time of tremendous change for both our people and the land. I wondered what she had felt and how she coped. I thought about the life of the collar—it would have been worn to ceremonies and treaty signings; it would have seen celebrations and days sadder than we can imagine; it would have heard generations speak our language, songs, and prayers—and then leave our community to sleep in a museum next to dance rattles without singers and with moccasins that would get up and dance if only someone would sound that rattle.

Who would have thought it would take three long years—I know I didn't. Some of it had to do with the chaos of everyday life and work, some with the changes that happened over that period of time, and some is just a mystery. There is a flow that happens when you're in the right space and frame of mind that many creative people experience. When it happens, it feels like something greater is working through you; you become "just the hands," and magic can happen. It can't be forced; when it comes, you have to be ready to get out of your own way and let it happen. I did try to speed things along by working during a really stressful time; the result was that I had to take out over eight hours of hand-stitched silk ribbon, because I had failed to notice a measuring error. After that, I let things move in their own time. Part of the mystery of letting things happen that way is that the beadwork and ribbon-work were finished on May 24, a day that has meaning to you and your mother, which I did not learn of until this morning as I was writing this. This was the day that she joined her ancestors.

I believe that we put a little of our spirit into all that we make, and it was important to me that this collar be made in a good way and in a good frame of mind. I prayed for strength, health, balance, peace, and all that is good for you and your family, for our ancestors, our people today, and all our tribal members who will be born in the future. I prayed for the earth, the land and the water, the air, the plants and trees, the salmon and all the fish, the animals, birds, amphibians, and insects, and all that is seen and unseen, known and unknown, that guides, helps, and protects us.

It was such an honor to make the collar for you. Thinking about the lives of our ancestors and relatives, your mother's life and all that she did for our community, your life and your courage and bravery at Omaha Beach gave me courage and strength to get through the times that seemed unbearable during the past couple of years. I have learned so much about faith and the will to keep on. I know the spirits are working behind the scenes to guide and help us, if we will only just listen. Woliwon, for giving me this opportunity; it was a gift that will live in my heart and spirit forever.

I hope that in a couple hundred years this collar will inspire one of our descendents to think deeply about her ancestors and to create something new. Sweetgrass will be burned, prayers will be said, and we will listen.

In love & spirit,
Jennifer Sapiel Neptune

Conclusion

In this book, I have tried to chronicle much of my life, spanning more than eight decades. Half of it was spent overseas, far from my ancestral homeland of the Penobscot Indian Nation. While my personal journey since the mid 1920s has been unique, it is also representative of many other Native Americans of my generation.

Like me, tens of thousands are veterans of foreign wars and have spent precious years far away from their tribal reservations. Many thousands have been wounded or killed overseas in service of our country, our freedom.

I have only briefly commented on my role as a medic in three wars, WWII, the Korean War, and the Cold War. When looking at my military medals, earned as a combat medic on the front, you will not see a Purple Heart.

While taking care of my fallen comrades, I myself was never wounded. I attribute my miraculous survival in combat to my mother's prayers and am grateful that it was my destiny to enjoy a long life with many blessings. Like many other Native American veterans, I married my foreign sweetheart and established a family overseas, before finally returning home again as a tribal elder, enjoying my final years on my own ancestral island in the Penobscot River.

As a personal memoir of how one Native son adventured, struggled, and persevered, my life history is now an open book. I hope my memories of sometimes difficult challenges and many exciting opportunities will be understood as a small part of a rich legacy of my ancient tribal nation in Maine.

Following the historical examples of our illustrious ancestors, we Penobscots have never forsaken our cultural heritage, and I trust that I have made my own contribution to ensure our survival as a proud Indian Nation in Maine.

May the reader enjoy and learn from our collective and individual histories. Woliwon!

Afterword

by James Eric Francis Sr.
Tribal Historian
Penobscot Nation

In 2001 Donna Loring, Penobscot Nation representative to the Maine State Legislature, introduced a bill called LD 0291. The 120th Maine Legislature passed the bill into law, thus becoming Maine State Law 2001, Chapter 403, An Act to Require Teaching of Maine Native American History and Culture in Maine's Schools. In a speech celebrating the passing of the law, Donna Loring stated that "through education comes understanding, and from understanding comes respect."

The Wabanaki Studies Commission was charged with implementing the law and recommending appropriate resources. It became clear that the best resources were to come from the Native American communities of Maine. The Wabanaki Studies Commission included members from the four Native American communities in Maine: Houlton Band of Maliseet Indians, Aroostook Band of Micmac, Passamaquoddy Tribe of Indians, and the Penobscot Nation. Each of these tribes began to find ways to ensure that the resources available were tribally correct and culturally appropriate.

The Penobscot Nation began developing curriculum and resources. They also looked to the Penobscot community for appropriate resources. What they found was a diverse Penobscot voice ready to help the population of Maine understand Penobscot people.

This publication, written by Charles Norman Shay, will be an honored addition to this increasingly growing list of resources. This book is the latest publication that Charles has personally guided. Charles's contribution has spanned three generations of the Nicolar/Shay family. In 2002 Charles acted as publisher of a biography of his Aunt Lucy Nicolar-Poolaw, *Princess Watahwaso: Bright Star of the Penobscot*. This history of his "Aunt Lu" was written by a good friend, Bunny McBride. In 2006 Charles had a companion book published, *Florence Nicolar Shay: Penobscot Basketmaker and Tribal Advocate*. This biography of Charles's mother, Florence, was written by Kate Kennedy. Charles felt it was important that the stories of these two incredible women be made available through these publications. In 2007, Charles

fully supported the republication of Joseph Nicolar's *The Life and Traditions of the Red Man*. Edited by Annette Kolodny, this book featured the 1893 version of Nicolar's book and also an introduction by Charles Norman Shay. Published by Duke University Press in 2007, this treasure of Native American literature has been reborn and is a respected resource embraced by the Penobscot Nation and universities across the United States. Joseph Nicolar was the father of both Lucy Nicolar-Poolaw and Florence Nicolar Shay, and grandfather to Charles Norman Shay. Without Charles's insistence and support, this book would not have been published and gained the readership it now has. Charles has given several talks on the publication of the original 1893 version and has written a presentation,

SCULPTURE OF JOSEPH NICOLAR BY TIM SHAY

The Life and Traditions of Joseph Nicolar, which was developed into a video by Charles Norman Shay. This video is a fine companion piece to the book by his grandfather.

Project Omaha Beach goes beyond his family, for Charles. This publication is a deeply personal look into the life of Charles Norman Shay. Being a humble man, this publication was hardest for Charles to write and have published. However, Charles recognizes that through his life and the accolades given to him, he can elevate the Native American veteran in this country. Through all these publications, Charles has ensured that the voice of his family and the Penobscot Nation is heard. Charles is also the founder and proprietor of Princess Watahwaso's Teepee: A Family Museum. This museum honors his family and is a monument to Charles's dedication and commitment to preserving the past and ensuring that the Penobscot people gain the respect that they deserve.

I have had the great honor of working with Charles on many projects over the past few years. This book is just a glimpse into the incredible man that I consider my friend.

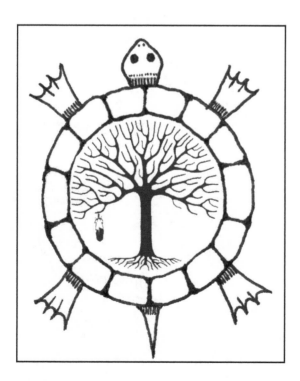

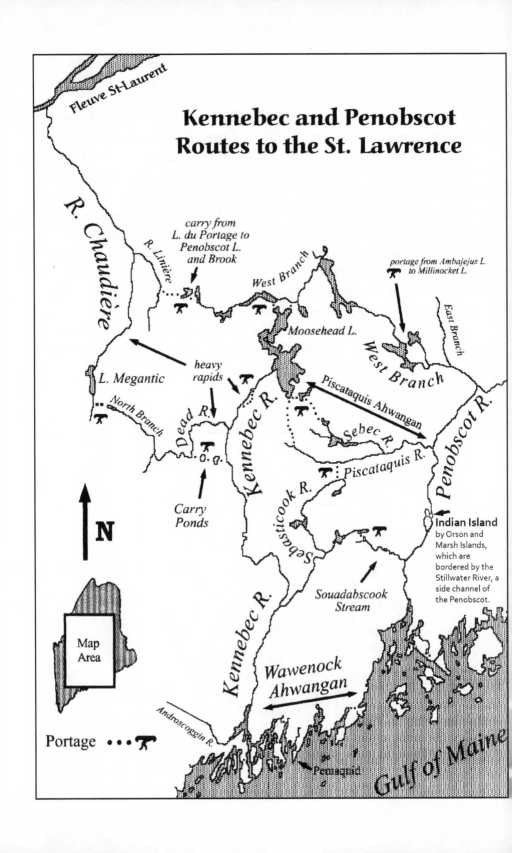

Kennebec and Penobscot Routes to the St. Lawrence

Fleuve St-Laurent

R. Chaudière

R. Linière

carry from
L. du Portage to
Penobscot L.
and Brook

West Branch

portage from Ambajejus L.
to Millinocket L.

East Branch

Moosehead L.

West Branch

heavy
rapids

L. Megantic

North Branch

Dead R.

Kennebec R.

Piscataquis Ahwangan

Sebec R.

Penobscot R.

Carry
Ponds

Sebasticook R.

Piscataquis R.

N

Indian Island
by Orson and
Marsh Islands,
which are
bordered by the
Stillwater River, a
side channel of
the Penobscot.

Map
Area

Souadabscook
Stream

Kennebec R.

Wawenock
Ahwangan

Androscoggin R.

Portage •••

Pemaquid

Gulf of Maine

Charles Norman Shay is a Penobscot Indian elder at Indian Island, Maine. Born in 1924, he enjoyed his childhood years living on this small island in the Penobscot River, opposite Old Town. He is the grandson of the author of *The Life and Traditions of the Red Man* (1893), Joseph Nicolar, and proud of his heritage. Reviewing his own long life, he decided to share his personal story as a result of a pilgrimage he made to Omaha Beach in 2007, more than sixty years after he waded ashore as a nineteen-year-old combat medic in a 1st Division assault platoon in the first wave of D-Day.

Although his regiment suffered about one thousand casualties on that day, Charles Shay was able to rescue many wounded comrades. For his heroic efforts on 6 June 1944, he earned a Silver Star.

After the Normandy campaign, Shay continued serving as a combat medic on the front, including the Battle of the Bulge. After crossing the Rhine, he became a prisoner of war but was liberated after several weeks in captivity.

Soon after returning home, he reenlisted and served as a medic with American occupation troops in Vienna, where he and his wife Lilli were married. In 1950, after leaving Austria, he was reassigned to the 3rd Division

and became a medic in the Korean War. He earned more medals and was promoted to master sergeant. After his honorable discharge and a brief return to Maine, Shay enlisted in the U.S. Air Force and was sent to the Central Pacific Ocean, where atomic bombs were tested.

In 1964, having retired from the military, the young Penobscot and his Austrian wife returned to Vienna, where he worked for the International Atomic Energy Agency and the Office of the United Nations High Commissioner for Refugees until 1988. Since then, Shay has returned to Indian Island, where he inherited the house and teepee that had belonged to his aunt Lucy, better known as Princess Watahwaso.

Since 2007, when he decided to return to the battlefields in Normandy, Belgium, and Germany, he has received much recognition for his contribution to the war effort, including the Legion of Honor from the French president. In this memoir, the author offers us a window into his personal life, so full of unexpected twists and turns that took him across the globe.

Prof. Harald E. L. Prins,
Dept. of Anthropology
Kansas State University

Scan

Interview with
Charles Norman Shay

CHARLESNORMANSHAY.COM

Induction ceremony
of Carole Duval

Life and Traditions of Joseph Nicolar
read by Charles Norman Shay

Contact Charles N. Shay
P.O. Box 65, Old Town, ME 04468
207 827-5744 CNSHAY@CHARLESNORMANSHAY.COM

Lightning Source UK Ltd.
Milton Keynes UK
UKHW010241161118
332417UK00001B/239/P